COLLEGE OF THE SEQUOIAS LIBRARY

D0977531

MUSCLES, SPEED & LIES

MUSCLES, SPEED & LIES

What the Sport Supplement Industry Does Not Want Athletes or Consumers to Know

DAVID LIGHTSEY, MS

THE LYONS PRESS
Guilford, Connecticut
AN IMPRINT OF THE GLOBE PEQUOT PRESS

The Lyons Press is an imprint of The Globe Pequot Press

10 9 8 7 6 5 4 3 2 1

Printed in the United States of America

DESIGNED BY CLAIRE ZOGHB

ISBN-13: 978-159228-912-7
ISBN-10: 1-59228-912-6

Library of Congress Cataloging-in-Publication Data is available on file.

CONTENTS

ACKNOWLEDGMENTS

IN ADDITION TO THE OBVIOUS GRATITUDE the author has to Tom McCarthy and The Lyons Press for the professional assistance and publishing I would also like to thank the editing assistance of Kathryn Thompson and Virginia Cowart. Lastly, I would like to thank the many very busy researchers and other professionals who are mentioned in the book who took the time over the years to respond to my inquiries and data collection, especially Jerry Attaway, past physical development coordinator for the San Francisco 49ers.

INTRODUCTION

According to the National Academies of Sciences, sales of supplements (there are approximately 29,000 products available, with 1,000 new products introduced each year) bring in more than $16 billion a year. Of this $16 billion, roughly $6.1 billion is spent on sport supplements that promise to enhance health, physical development, or performance. For the past 16 years, with the National Council Against Health Fraud (NCAHF), Quackwatch, and working in the sports medicine and physical rehabilitation field, I have answered countless questions from educators, patients, news media, consumers, athletes, coaches, professional athletic organizations, and parents regarding these purported health and physical enhancement benefits, as well as related questions on sports nutrition. Most supplement inquiries involve claims that are just blatantly false and silly, but many involve products with some significant potential for harm. Many of these products actually do more to hinder development than to enhance it. Given the limited nutrition science education of most people, it is easy to understand why so many are so easily deceived or misled by the persuasive and clever advertising or promotional hype. Most educators, athletes, and consumers are simply unprepared to navigate through this quagmire of misinformation. Legislatures, and high school and collegiate governing bodies now recognize the need for more oversight of this industry—and that more must be done to protect consumers.

Muscles, Speed & Lies provides educators, coaches, parents, consumers, and athletes the information they need to not only objectively cut through all the hype but it will also help to develop an understanding of basic nutrition needed to make the relevant dietary changes most athletes and active consumers typically need.

At present, most people can't accurately answer some simple questions about general nutrition, dietary supplements, the food supply process, and the purported health benefits of things such as, for example, supplemental "antioxidants."

How much of the purported health benefits or threats are true?

To what extent are these claims based upon good science?

Is there a downside to any of this?

Most consumers, athletes, and educators can't provide adequate answers to these questions, as well as many others, because they are not trained to. And the supplement industry takes advantage of this lack of training. Read this book and the problem will be resolved.

Muscles, Speed & Lies illustrates the extent this industry relies upon misleading or false advertising. It also provides the objective scientific information to clarify for readers why the sport supplement industry must operate in this manner to maintain their markets, and why it is unnecessary to purchase the vast majority of their products if some simple dietary guidelines were followed.

Muscles, Speed & Lies also shows that the vast majority of the sports supplement marketplace has been fabricated by very clever but deceptive marketing practices. There simply would not be a demand for most products if a false need had not been created. Consumer demand for most products is based on misunderstandings—and the supplement industry is very much aware that all it has to do is exploit these misunderstandings.

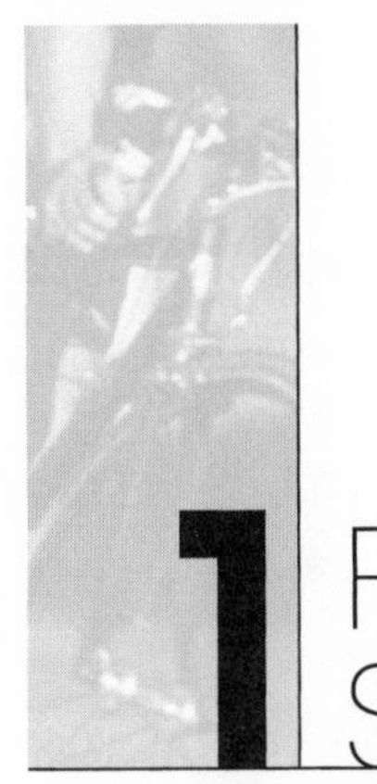

1 FLEECING AND SWINDLING

DECEPTION IN THE SUPPLEMENT INDUSTRY

"They can get your urine and blood and prescribe a vitamin specifically for your blood type and what your body needs." While this statement might sound silly to someone with a degree in the medical or health sciences, it is a common misconception among many athletes and active consumers.

It's not surprising that so many consumers embrace the claims of the dietary and sports supplement industries. Most simply do not have the background or training to objectively separate the hype—perpetuated by millions of dollars in advertising each year—from the facts. But even professional athletes fall prey to the marketing tactics of supplement companies; in fact, the statement quoted above came from a high-profile Major League Baseball player in an October 5, 2004, FoxSports.com news report.

Even more surprising is how many formally trained sports medicine or physical development professionals perpetuate the myths and misconceptions behind dietary and sport supplements, in lectures, magazine or journal articles, trade books, and even popular college-level health textbooks. Consider the three examples below from a college health textbook, a peer review journal article, and a sports nutrition trade book intended for the general consumer market. All three mistakenly state that the water-soluble vitamins are not stored. This information is typically why so many athletes feel they need to take a daily supplement of vitamins, such as vitamin C, in order to maintain appropriate levels of these nutrients. Vitamin C has a storage capacity of 1,500 milligrams, a fact few athletes or consumers are aware of.

1. The peer reviewed *National Strength and Conditioning Association Journal* published for professionals states, "The water-soluble vitamins (B complex, C, and the bioflavonoids) are absorbed directly into the bloodstream *and are not stored in the body [my emphasis]*. For this reason it is important to replenish them daily." ("The Reinvention of Nutrition Basics," Anthony A. D'Assis. *NSCA Performance Training Journal*, Volume 2, No. 5, pg. 11).
2. The college level textbook *An Invitation to Health.* "The B vitamins and vitamin C are water-soluble; they are absorbed directly into the blood then used up or washed out of the body in urine or sweat. *They must be replaced daily [my emphasis]."* (*An Invitation to Health,* 10th Edition, Instructor's Edition, Thomas Wadsworth Publisher, pg. 1,520). This is not a publisher issue necessarily but a common mistake by many authors. The same publisher's college level nutrition text, which I use as an adjunct instructor, contains the correct information.
3. The trade book *Fuel for Young Athletes* states, *"They can not be stored in the body" [my emphasis]* when referring to the water-soluble vitamins (*Fuel for Young Athletes,* Human Kinetics, pg. 12, 2004).

Keep in mind that I am not stating that the above resources are not good, I am just pointing out a common mistake even among professionals in the field. I personally own the college health textbook as well as the trade book.

In short, millions of people believe that the physical demands they make on their bodies require the support of supplements. And the supplement industry—with $13 billion to $16 billion in annual revenues, reaching $6.1 billion in 2005 for sports supplements, excluding sales through Wal-Mart (MarketResearch.com, 10/1/05 report)—does much to foster that belief. In 1989 I began coordinating the National Council Against Health Fraud's (NCAHF) task force on ergogenic aids and athletic performance. The team's purpose was to assess the performance enhancement claims made by supplement companies for their products. To make an evaluation, we obtained the product, company promotional material, and advertising claims; reviewed the available data; and interviewed researchers and company spokespersons. Whenever possible, we compiled information about the product from peer-reviewed journals.

I have since reviewed the claims of more than one hundred companies and have become all too familiar with the deceptive marketing methods used most frequently by manufacturers to sell purported ergogenic aids. In 1992 the task force published the data we had collected on forty-five companies in the *National Strength and Conditioning Association Journal* (Volume 14; Issue 2, pp. 26–31, 1992). What was most striking about the report was that not *one* of the forty-five companies examined could provide credible, published, peer-reviewed scientific data to support its product's purported benefits! Sadly, we concluded that objective information about the role of supplements in physical development or athletic training is not likely to come from the supplement industry.

Now, of course, dietary supplements have become big business in the nonathletic population too. Consumers believe they can get all the nutrients they need by taking a commercial supplement.

Most also believe what is printed on the box or jar of supplements. Never has the saying "Let the buyer beware" had more relevance.

Dishonest supplement manufacturers have mastered a plethora of deceptive marketing methods, including:

- misrepresenting clinical studies,
- false, exaggerated, or purchased endorsements,
- unreliable testimonials,
- patent misrepresentation,
- media distortion and false advertising,
- seals of approval,
- RDAs taken out of context, and
- erroneous assertions.

In the *New York State Journal of Medicine* (2; 1993), Sarah Short, PhD, of Syracuse University, said, "[E]ven the most informed athletes may not be able to calculate the risk-to-benefit ratio of the newest product hitting the market nor care about the long-term effects." Nevertheless, athletes and active consumers who learn to recognize the industry's false claims of health and performance enhancement will be less vulnerable to this kind of deception, protecting both their pocketbooks and their long-term health.

Misrepresenting Clinical Studies

Misrepresentation of research is a far-reaching category that includes the following techniques:

- taking research results out of context or extrapolating results beyond what the original research demonstrated,
- fabricating research or omitting relevant facts to give the impression that science supports a claim,
- falsely claiming a product has been "university tested,"
- falsely claiming to be conducting "double-blind research,"
- stating that the research is "not for public review," and
- inappropriately referencing research results.

TAKING RESEARCH OUT OF CONTEXT OR EXTRAPOLATING BEYOND THE ORIGINAL RESEARCH

In 2004 the U.S. House of Representatives and the U.S. Senate passed the Anabolic Steroid Act prohibiting the over-the-counter sale of the weak anabolic precursors androstenedione and reclassified it as a controlled substance. Precursors are any compound that can be converted into another. Androstenedione can be converted into either testosterone or estrogen. Although androstenedione is no longer on the market, it provides a perfect example of why athletes and consumers should not rely on the sport supplement industry to provide honest information about products or to protect their health. Consumers must remember, it has literally taken an act of Congress to restrain this industry.

In July 1998 Arty Berko of ESPN's *Outside-the-Lines* asked me to review the claims for Andro-6, an androstenedione-based product marketed by Experimental Applied Science (EAS) of Golden, Colorado, and made famous by Mark McGwire. On its Web site in 1998, EAS claimed that Andro-6 would "boost your testosterone the legal way." It called Andro-6 "the scientifically designed precision androgenic support complex" and claimed that through a "blend of six unique nutrients," the product would "naturally reinforce testosterone levels" "thereby decreasing the likelihood of estrogen-related side effects like gynecomastia."

After reviewing the "science" behind Andro-6, I concluded that of seventeen studies EAS provided, only *one* was relevant, and that study actually demonstrated possible safety concern for Andro-6 because the study indicated that it did raise testosterone levels. However the study was conducted on women in 1992 and was unrelated to males or muscle development (*ACTA Endocrinologica* 41, 1962 400–406, "The In Vivo Conversion of Dehydroepiandrosterone and Androstenedione to Testosterone in the Human"). I sent a summary of my findings to ESPN, including this statement: "It is my opinion that all but one of these studies is being completely extrapolated beyond what the study demonstrates. This is not a 'health food' supplement. Anyone taking this compound assuming that it is without potential significant risks is either very foolish or poorly educated in the sciences . . . . [I]t is my opinion that any manufacturer selling DHEA or androstenedione over-the-counter is strictly motivated by greed and has absolutely no regard for the health of those who purchase these drugs."

In support of my position consider the comments made by Samuel S. C. Yen, M.D., D.SC., a W.R. Person Professor of Reproductive Medicine at the University of California, San Diego. In 1998 I asked Dr. Yen to comment on EAS use of a research paper he published in the *Journal of Clinical Endocrinology and Metabolism* in 1990, as well as a book chapter in the Annals of the New York Academy of Science titled "DHEA and Aging" (pp. 128–142), to promote the utilization of Andro-6.

Dr. Yen on August 25, 1998 faxed the following comment to my office. "Statements made by EAS are clearly out of context, highly inappropriate and misleading."

ESPN in turn asked Gary Wadler, American College of Sports Medicine physician, member of the World Anti-Doping Agency (WADA), and an international authority on doping in sports, to review the research EAS sent to my office in support of its claims. Dr. Wadler stated definitively, "I would give an F to any medical student who used the scientific data and came to the conclusion they reached. I would give an F to any doctor who treated patients based upon the utilization of the facts, given the way those facts were twisted, distorted, and turned."

> *Expert Input*
>
> **March 2000 statements by the Endocrine Society, which comprises more than 8,500 scientists and physicians in seventy-two countries who study and test the endocrine system. (http://www.endo-society.org/news/press/2000/20000201.cfm).**

> Androstenedione is a steroid. In the body, it is converted to testosterone. It can also be converted into the female sex steroid, estrogen, in boys and girls.
>
> Androstenedione cannot be a dietary supplement since it is not part of the normal diet.
>
> The body has its own wisdom. Too much androgen shuts off the body's own production of testosterone. This can impair normal testicular function—"it shrinks your grapes to raisins."
>
> The use of androgens is especially dangerous among adolescents in whom it MIGHT stunt growth.
>
> The purity of commercial Andro is unknown, unregulated, and probably varies widely. The user of Andro has no way of knowing what he or she is taking.
>
> At present, it is not known whether Andro is safe or effective. For these reasons, the Endocrine Society believes that more research is needed before any use of this agent can be recommended.

The October 1998 *Pharmacist's Letter*, an online subscription service for pharmacists covering developments in drug therapy, urged pharmacists to "caution people that androstenedione might cause the same problems as anabolic steroids . . . acne, mood swings, liver toxicity, heart attacks, and stunted growth in teens" (*Pharmacist's Letter*, Vol. 14, No. 10, October 1998).

The opinions expressed above are just a sampling from the medical literature, which had called for the removal of steroid precursors from the marketplace. Oddly enough, dehydroepiandrostenedione or DHEA as is normally stated on the labels, a precursor to androstenedione, remains readily available. The August 2005 U.C. Berkeley *Wellness Letter* published the following, which may explain why.

> *Congress deliberately exempted it (DHEA)—not because it is so different from the supplements just taken off the shelves, and*

> *certainly not with an eye to the health of the American public, but because its manufacturers wield plenty of political clout. According to the* New York Times, *DHEA sales amounted to $47 million in 2003. This steroid is marketed just as andro was ("beat fat, build muscle, increase sex drive!"), but is often pitched to older people as a means of staying youthful. Indeed, its chief protector in Congress, Senator Orrin Hatch of Utah, has cited it as an "anti-aging" pill. "It has given health and vigor to millions," the senator wrote in the* New York Times, *repeating the claims of the National Nutritional Foods Association. This industry group employs Scott Hatch, the senator's son, as a lobbyist (UC Berkeley* Wellness Letter, *August 2005, pg. 2).*

Ironically, an American College of Cardiology (ACC) News Release entitled "DHEA Linked to Early Signs of Atherosclerosis," pointed out that DHEA "may promote the formation of fatty plaques in arteries, according to a new laboratory study in the December 3, 2003 issue of the *Journal of the American College of Cardiology.*" The study was conducted on laboratory cell cultures and not actual patients, so the report states, "It does not address what may happen when the body converts DHEA into testosterone or estrogen." However, the ACC cautioned, "This adds to the growing evidence that anabolic steroids or precursors thereof, such as DHEA, may have detrimental effects on cardiovascular health." (ACC News Release, 12/2/03).

A 2002 report in *The Physician and Sportsmedicine* (2000:2) proclaimed that anabolic steroid use among eighth-grade boys rose from 1.6 percent in 1998 to 2.5 percent in 1999. As have many others, the senior researcher at the University of Michigan Institute for Social Research, quoted in the article, suggested that the reported use of androstenedione by high-profile athletes has diminished the safety concerns for many young athletes.

In another example, in 1987 a number of supplement companies began claiming that boron was an anabolic (muscle-building) agent, based on USDA studies in postmenopausal women (Nielson, F. et al. 1987; "Effects of dietary boron on mineral, estrogen, and testosterone metabolism in postmenopausal women." *FASEB Journal* 1:394–397). In this study, researchers examined the effectiveness of aluminum, magnesium, and boron on major mineral metabolism in postmenopausal women and concluded that supplementing a low-boron diet with an amount of boron that could be found in diets high in fruits and vegetables can help prevent osteoporosis in older women. The study had nothing to do with muscle mass development. However, this same study also happened to show that a daily boron dosage of 3 milligrams a day increased testosterone in postmenopausal women from 0.3 to 0.6 nanograms per milliliter. A number of supplement companies quickly began promoting boron as a natural anabolic agent, even though the normal level of male testosterone is approximately ten times that observed in the USDA study, and the test subjects were women in their fifties and sixties. One supplement firm told me by phone that if boron increases testosterone in these women *at all*, it must be an effective anabolic agent. This is comparable to marketing a mouse as an elephant.

FABRICATING RESEARCH OR OMITTING RELEVANT FACTS

An article in the December 2003 *Muscle & Fitness Magazine* entitled "Keto Crazed" promoted the purported anabolic effects of a low-carbohydrate diet for bodybuilders. The author, a professor in the Human Performance Laboratory at the University of Connecticut, Storrs, stated that "six weeks of a very low-carbohydrate diet with adequate calories not only decreased body fat but *also increased muscle mass (by almost 3 pounds) in normal-weight men. And these guys never even picked up a weight*" [my emphasis]. I found this claim impossible to believe, and I contacted the author to request the data he used to support such a wild claim.

The author sent me a copy of his original research paper, which he had published in the journal *Metabolism* (Vol. 51, No. 7, July 2002, pp. 864–870). Under the subject heading "Material and Methods," the paper stated that "subjects were moderately active performing a variety of different aerobic and *weight-training routines*" and that "in the carbohydrate restricted diet group, 1 subject was sedentary, 5 performed regular aerobic exercise (2 to 4 times/wk for 20 to 60 minutes), and *6 performed a combination of aerobic exercise (3 to 5 times/wk for 15 to 90 minutes) and resistance exercise (2 to 6 times/wk for 45 to 120 minutes)*" [my emphasis]. These facts, an obvious contradiction of the *Muscle & Fitness Magazine* article, clearly explain how the participants gained a half-pound of muscle mass per week—a normal rate of development in previously untrained individuals early in their training programs.

While one researcher's work can easily be distorted by another, in this case the author of the fabricated information in the *Muscle & Fitness* article was also the main author of the published research paper. In fact, it's not that unusual to see individuals misrepresent their own work in both science journals and lay publications. By omitting the subjects' weight-training regimens from the magazine article, the author suggested the implausible and misled thousands of readers (The American Council on Science and Health listed *Muscle & Fitness* as a poor source of health information in its January 2004 publication *Nutrition Accuracy in Popular Magazines*.)

"UNIVERSITY TESTED"

Some companies have reported positive university research that was never conducted, or have fabricated the actual results. A 1989 report in *Muscle & Fitness* magazine stated that a study conducted at

San Diego State University had demonstrated the effectiveness of amino acid supplement products compared to controls that took no supplements; the television series *Inside Edition* on 3/10/1989 (KCBS-TV/CH. 2) revealed that the research was never conducted.

In June 1991 the magazine *Triathlete* ran a six-page advertisement for the product Enerzymes CAPS. On the third page of the advertisement it stated in bold large type "Scientific Proof Positive From a Major University." The advertisement also went on to boldly name where the study was conducted, Fresno State University, as well as the professor involved, which made it easy to validate if the claims were true. The professor, Tim Anderson Ed.D., Director of the Human Performance Lab, forwarded a copy of the study to my office. The authors of the study stated in the abstract "It was concluded that there would be no physiological benefit associated with use of these supplements."

"CURRENTLY DOING DOUBLE-BLIND RESEARCH"

This common statement is rarely true. When manufacturers are asked to provide documentation supporting their ergogenic aid claims, they often provide this response in lieu of real details about their research, such as the number or type of subjects, principle investigator, facility or university testing the product, length of study, and so on. This sudden lapse of memory is a sure sign of intentional evasiveness.

"RESEARCH NOT FOR PUBLIC REVIEW"

Claiming that research is "not for public review" is another dodge that should be a red flag. Athletes and consumers have the right to review objective documentation about manufacturers' performance or health claims. There is no rational reason for supplement manufacturers not to be open if positive publishable proof of their claims exists.

INAPPROPRIATELY REFERENCED RESEARCH

Inappropriately referenced research is such a far-reaching problem that it's been categorized into five types: unpublished, Eastern European, poorly controlled, outdated, and not peer-reviewed. **Unpublished data** is similar to research "not for public review," but unpublished data can sometimes be obtained from companies. However, the data is typically so poorly controlled or used such poor research methods that no conclusions can be drawn from the work. This poor research quality explains why this type of work is not published; it is simply not acceptable to peer-reviewed journals.

Eastern European research is often based on hearsay, and details are unavailable. There is a myth that the physical training regimens of the former Communist bloc countries of Eastern Europe are somehow uniquely effective. We now know that some Eastern European countries did experiments on improving athletic performance but that many of the methods were dangerous and a number of former athletes suffered health consequences. Moreover, since there has been significant steroid use in Eastern European sports, as there has been in all developed countries, no direct cause-and-effect relationship between these training methods and performance can be established.

In **poorly controlled research** studies, it is impossible to establish a direct cause-and-effect relationship between a particular compound and the research outcome. The following is only a partial list of the sorts of variables that must be controlled in human studies: subject's age, gender, body composition, training or conditioning status, motivation or mental state, diet, hydration; exercise type, duration, intensity, frequency; weather; clothing/equipment changes; length of the study; competency of the researcher.

Sometimes **outdated or old research** that showed positive results is used to back a claim even when newer, better-controlled research that has negative results is available.

Purported clinical studies can also be deceptive if the material is not peer-reviewed before it is published. "Peer-reviewed" simply means that an article was read closely by several scientists in the same field to judge its accuracy and scientific worth before publication. Such expert review is designed to prevent shoddy or incomplete work from being published, but it certainly is not a perfect system. Studies that have not been reviewed before publication may appear in popular magazines or by direct distribution to the consumer. It is easy to fabricate scientific sounding and appearing data with elaborate manipulated graphs and charts, which can then be inserted in marketing material, mailed directly to the consumer, published in a magazine, or posted on a Web page to make it appear objective and scientific.

False, Exaggerated, or Purchased Endorsements

Some products appear to have the backing of professional organizations, universities, or elite athletes. While some product endorsements are legitimate, the smart consumer will consider these statements with a healthy degree of suspicion. An endorsement would be a written approval or the use of their name in advertising by a respected organization, which in turn would automatically add credibility to the product. This slightly differs from a testimonial, which is also a verbal or written endorsement but within the context of this book will only refer to an individual and not any organization as a whole.

In some cases, a manufacturer implies that an entire team or sports organization endorses a product, when in fact it has not. For instance, in 1989 one firm claimed that the New York Yankees were among the organizations backing organic germanium as a performance-enhancement supplement. When the Yankee organization became aware that its name was being used without authorization, Michael Luczkovich, the executive V.P. and CEO at the time sent the supplement company a letter demanding it stop using the team name immediately. "The New York Yankee organization does not intend to either directly or indirectly endorse your product. I would suggest that you cease using our good name immediately. The Yankees will do everything under the law to protect its name and reputation."

Coach and trainer endorsements can also be misused and applied to entire teams or programs. In 1991 ex-Olympic swim coaches allowed the use of their names and professional positions as past Olympic swim coaches to market a supplement called BioSyn—despite the fact that the claims were not supported by any published, double-blind, peer-reviewed studies. With liberal references to "U.S. Swimming," the company's promotional material would imply to many athletes that it had the organization's endorsement. In response to my query to U.S. Swimming regarding the accuracy of the claims made by BioSyn references to U.S. Swimming in their promotional material, Bernard J. Favaro, U.S. Swimming secretary and General Counsel at the time, stated that "U.S. Swimming will cooperate in every way possible to make sure that BioSyn does not claim endorsement of its products by U.S. Swimming, or its national teams, or its coaches as a group."

In 1997 I received a packet of information about a supplement company promoting its product PRO-HGH, which it claimed elevated levels of human growth hormone. The first line of the letter said, "The reason that the San Diego Chargers starting using PRO-HGH almost immediately after it became available three months ago was their belief that it could give the Chargers a substantial edge." A phone call to the Chargers' physical development coordinator at the time, John Hastings, quickly proved my assumption that the company was making a false claim. Hastings had never heard of the product, and what's more, he told me that he does not give supplements to his players.

Misinformation about sports supplements occasionally filters into legitimate educational clinics. This usually happens when a guest speaker promotes a product in such a way that some listeners believe the sponsoring organization is an endorser. At a U.S. Cycling Federation (USCF)–sponsored clinic at Bakersfield (California) Junior College in 1989, a guest speaker promoted the use of the supplements carnitine, inosine, octacosanol, arginine, ornithine, and dimethylglycine to enhance athletic performance—despite the absence of peer-reviewed, objective research material. A number of participants assumed the USCF agreed with the speaker's misinterpretation of the literature. When the USCF became aware of the problem, it quickly took measures to prevent a recurrence. Specifically, in January 1989, Chuck Wells, the development program manager at the time for the United States Cycling Federation sent out a letter to all regional coaching coordinators. In this letter he stated, "Because the clinics you perform are done under the auspices of the USCF, and material that you may present may be viewed by the attendees as being material endorsed by the UCSF we ask that you err on the conservative side . . . furthermore, we cannot emphasize strongly enough that if you represent any product featured in your presentation it will be viewed as a conflict of interest and will be dealt with in a most severe manner."

Some endorsements are legitimately purchased from a well-recognized athletic organization. While this type of business relationship enhances the profit margins of both organizations, I believe it is unethical on the part of sports organizations charged with maintaining scientific accountability and responsibility in the education and safety of athletes. The United States Olympic Committee, for example, has reportedly established marketing arrangements with several supplement manufacturers. For a fee, these companies have permission to use the Olympic Rings symbol on their promotional materials—a clear attempt to associate maximum athletic performance with use of the supplement, and to influence young athletes to try the product.

As an example, in October 1995 the supplement company Interior Design Nutritionals (IDN), a division of Nu Skin International, sent a letter to the San Francisco 49ers head coach George Seifert promoting their sports nutrition system to increase energy, reduce muscle fatigue, and accelerate recovery. Within this letter it states "Overdrive [which contains chromium picolinate as one of the ingredients], an IDN product endorsed by the United States Olympic Committee, is used and endorsed by many world class athletes." The coach had no interest in the product and I simply became aware of it because Jerry Attaway, the physical development coordinator at the time for the 49ers, forwarded the information to my office.

On the title page of the advertisement, which was included with the letter to Coach Seifert, it stated at the top, "IDN and the 1996 Olympics!" The first paragraph read, "IDN is an official licensee of the United States Olympic Committee (USOC) with 2 of our products, meaning that the USOC picked our products over hundreds of other competitors."

The third paragraph stated, "We are working with Olympic athletes Florence Griffith Joyner, Al Joyner, Pablo Morales, and Cathy Turner in marketing these products. And the entire U.S. Olympic team is using them as well." All four athletes mentioned above were prominently displayed in IDN's catalogue at that time.

A CHRONOLOGICAL REVIEW OF THE USOC/IDN ISSUE

- 1994—IDN licensee agreement with the USOC Sports Nutrition System.
- 1995—First FTC settlement with IDN parent company Nu Skin.
- 1995—I filed a formal complaint with the USOC Associate General Counsel Bert Fainberg as well as executive director of

the USOC Dick Schultz outlining the lack of safety and efficacy studies for the products.

- 1997—Nu Skin settled with the FTC for false advertising (see Chapter 2 for more details).
- 1999—Research presented at the American Chemical Society meeting in Anaheim, California indicating chromium picolinate may damage the DNA (animal study).

With all fairness to the USOC scientific and physical development staff, I am not aware of any staff member that I have had contact with over the years who would endorse these products. It appeared to be strictly business and a mutually financially beneficial agreement.

Consider the following partial reprint of a report provided by Selena Roberts in the January 20, 2002, *New York Times* entitled "Olympics: Athletes Guess on Supplements":

> *Pavle Jovanovic was not unlike many Olympic athletes who begin and end their training sessions taking nutritional supplements in an effort to maximize their body's potential.*
>
> *But at some point, Jovanovic says, he unknowingly ingested a multivitamin, nutrition bar or protein powder that contained traces of the steroid norandrostenedione, resulting in a positive drug test at the Olympic trials in December. On Sunday, Jovanovic was disqualified as a pusher on a United States Olympic bobsled team with gold medal potential at the Salt Lake City Games.*
>
> *He is appealing, but whatever the outcome, Jovanovic's case illuminates the contradictory and, to some critics, hypocritical messages American Olympic officials send their athletes. While leaders of the United States Anti-Doping Agency have bluntly told the athletes, "Do not take a vitamin and put it in your mouth, period," some critics believe the United States Olympic Committee and the Salt Lake Organizing Committee have undermined*

that message by granting sponsorships to companies that market supplements.

Last year, a report commissioned by the International Olympic Committee revealed that a quarter of the 600 over-the-counter nutritional supplements that were analyzed contained nonlabeled banned substances that could lead to a positive drug test. Yet an article on how to maximize resistance training with supplements was featured in a U.S.O.C. publication last fall: it recommended that various carbohydrate and protein drinks, mixes and shakes available on the commercial market could be consumed after a workout to "increase the amount of anabolic hormones in the body."

"It's a mixed message," Adam Driggs, a lawyer representing Jovanovic, said. "The I.O.C. isn't saying which manufacturers have supplements coming up in that 20 percent. They're worried about liability. It's about the almighty dollar."

Two years ago, the U.S.O.C. and Salt Lake organizers signed a deal through 2004 valued at $20 million with Nu Skin, a Utah based company, to supply Olympic training centers with supplements from its subsidiary, Pharmanex. There is no evidence that Pharmanex has produced anything other than pure products.

Pharmanex is not the only company making and distributing nutritional supplements that is associated with American Olympic teams. Advocare is a sponsor of the bobsled federation, and the American speed skating team lists Usana Health Science as a corporate supporter.

In Jovanovic's case, Dr. Donald Catlin, director of the I.O.C.'s drug-testing lab at UCLA, testified on his behalf at a hearing last Friday. Catlin said that the metabolites in Jovanovic's system were most likely from a contaminated supplement and provided no competitive advantage.

In September 1998 the law firm of Dow, Lohnes and Albertson of Washington D.C., representing *USA Today*, notified Serotril Sciences

International regarding their unauthorized use of the *USA Today* name. The letter stated that the advertising brochure, "Implies that *USA Today* has reported on the Serotril Product . . . our client is not aware of an *USA Today* story regarding Serotril. In addition, our client has never sponsored or endorsed the Serotril product. Furthermore, your misleading advertisement constitutes false advertisement and is a violation of federal and state law."

Some scientific organizations contribute to misinformation and misconceptions as well. However, some professional organizations are speaking out against these kinds of marketing arrangements as unethical. Tommy Boone, editor in chief of the American Society of Exercise Physiologists (ASEP) *Journal of Exercise Physiology*, has said, "Frankly, I forced four ASEP board members off the board after realizing they were using ASEP to front their supplement products. It is not possible to do that kind of thing and build a professional organization" (e-mail to the author, 8/19/04).

In a practice that should be of particular concern to parents sending a child off to college to play sports, it has become common for individuals within university athletic departments to collaborate with supplement companies. The athletic department provides a positive spin on the performance-enhancing properties of a company's products and in turn increases income for the school's often financially strapped programs.

The April 7, 2003, issue of *Sports Illustrated* highlighted the growing link between many university athletic departments and the sports supplement industry. In my opinion, this is an unethical alliance unless the university can prove a direct benefit to the athlete that cannot be provided by a good diet alone and that the products are safe and not contaminated.

Unreliable Testimonials

Testimonials are among the oldest and most popular selling techniques. They are simply a written personal statement or verbal comment testifying, falsely or truthfully, to the value of the product. When an elite athlete swears he relies on Brand X, sales will soar. But the perceptive consumer knows that testimonials can be faked, bought, or embellished by editing. Even when the individual is providing a truthful testimonial, the benefit he or she describes may be due to natural improvement, the placebo effect, or a wide variety of altered training or dietary habits, which occurred simultaneously.

The placebo effect is very real. Research has shown that 30 percent to 40 percent of subjects taking an inert pill or powder will claim to have experienced a benefit from it or will actually *demonstrate* a measurable positive response in mental or physical performance. In either case, the response is easily attributable to the fulfilling of expectations that can develop from a good marketing pitch and the resulting psychological impact this motivating factor can have in training. This is generally believed to occur through the increased production of endorphins, which is temporary and wanes after the initial anticipated changes.

In an editorial published in the journal *Headache*, John Meads M.D. stated, "Placebos are catalysts for the transformation of expectations to effects. Positive expectations may evoke positive effects, negative expectations may evoke no effects, or adverse effects." (*Headache*, November 1984, pp. 342–343). This was beautifully illustrated in a 1972 study in which six selected experienced weightlifters were led to believe that they had qualified to receive anabolic steroids (Dianabol) under close supervision. The lifters actually received placebos. The results were striking, with the athletes showing strength gains beyond reasonable progression (Ariel, Gideon, Saville, William. "Anabolic steroids: the physiological effects of placebos." *Medicine and Science in Sports and Exercise*; 4:124–126). This study demonstrated that even experienced athletes are not immune to the placebo effect.

Joy Bunt, PhD, cites another good example of the placebo effect that she observed some years ago. While working at the Department of Exercise and Sport Science at the University of Arizona, Dr. Bunt was evaluating the effects on human growth hormone and strength of the amino acids arginine and lysine. She studied two comparable groups of athletes who received either the amino acids or a cornstarch placebo. Neither group knew which substance they were taking. At the end of the study, both groups were about equal in strength. However, one of the athletes in the placebo group did experience strength changes and refused to believe he had been taking cornstarch. Had this athlete been given the opportunity to present his opinion to his peers, he would have given a favorable testimonial for cornstarch.

The cost of this subjective deception for some athletes can be significant. On September 28, 2002, the *Sydney Morning Herald* reported, "Australia's Olympic medallist Cathy Freeman spent $3,480 on vitamins and supplements from health food shops in the four months leading up to the Sydney Olympic Games."

Natural improvement, especially in untrained athletes, can easily lead consumers to believe a product helped their performance. This most often occurs when an athlete begins taking a product just prior to the point in training at which he or she would normally experience some natural improvements. The only way to objectively attribute any positive gains to a specific product or ingredient is to conduct a double-blind study. Without objective published data, a testimonial is only a reflection of the motivation that was inspired by faith in a particular supplement.

Here's another, humorous example of the placebo effect at work. An endocrinologist I was working with years ago asked me to examine the supplements being taken by one of her patients. The physician wanted to be sure the patient was not taking anything that could add to her current medical problems. On her next visit, the patient emptied the contents of a grocery bag onto the exam table, revealing twenty to twenty-five bottles of supplements she routinely took "for her health." She confidently rattled off all the benefits for approximately ten of the products. Then she paused and stared at the items on the table, not saying a word for several moments. When she finally looked at me, she said, "I take one of these to help my memory, but I can't remember which one it is!" I could only laugh, and so did she when she realized the product's apparent ineffectiveness. Up until this point, she had assumed she was benefiting from these products and thus had subjectively determined that they had improved her health.

These examples show that many people need only a little help in self-deception. Once they succumb to the clever but deceptive claims of a particular product, they are far more likely to put in the extra effort required for a short time to obtain positive results. Unfortunately, this extra effort will eventually wane, leaving the consumer ready for another fleecing.

Patent Misrepresentation

Consumers often incorrectly assume that if a product has been granted a patent number, the U.S. Patent Office must have deemed it effective. Actually, the Patent Office does not concern itself with the effectiveness of a product, only with its distinguishable differences from other products. What's more, a patent can be obtained based only on a theoretical model and does not have to be backed up with objective double-blind research. The mention of a patent in promotional copy can be nothing more than a marketing gimmick.

2 MEDIA DISTORTIONS AND FALSE ADVERTISING

Manufacturers market their dubious ergogenic aids by mass media methods of all kinds, including both paid advertising and unpaid-for publicity coverage. Advertising has limited First Amendment protection, and false or misleading advertising claims are subject to prosecution by the Federal Trade Commission. (False product labeling for drugs falls under the jurisdiction of the Food and Drug Administration, but supplements are not by definition either food or drug and therefore are loosely regulated by the FDA.)

Publicity can be much harder to recognize than paid advertising. It can take the form of editorial comment, feature articles, talk-show interviews, and planted "news" stories. Materials that extol a product's benefits but do not bear any company identification often are advertising masquerading as publicity. These types of communication enjoy greater First Amendment protection than paid ads. Even so, those responsible for them are vulnerable to prosecution if a conspiracy to deceive the public to sell a specific product can be proven. Unfortunately, violators tend to be ignored unless they pose a substantial danger to the public or some other reason to attract attention from busy regulators.

A good rule to keep in mind is that when a product claims to prevent, alleviate, or cure a physical or mental disorder, or to alter the structure or function of the body (altering muscle structure, for example), it should be classified as a drug and thus subject to premarketing approval by the FDA. If the FDA does not approve such a substance, be on your guard.

Seals of Approval

Some companies now utilize various "seals of approval" from independent nonprofit laboratories to lend their products credibility. Sally Squires of the *Washington Post* described this technique in a December 4, 2001, article entitled "Making a Claim on Credibility—New Plan Will Verify Some Supplements' Claims But Not Safety, Efficacy." Squires stated that several organizations, including the United States Pharmacopoeia (USP), the Good Housekeeping Institute, ConsumerLab.com, and NSF International, had "programs underway to review the manufacturing practices of supplement makers and evaluate ingredients in products." If a manufacturer meets a given organization's criteria for label accuracy in terms of content purity and declared amounts such as specific milligrams or ounces, it can use that organization's seal of approval on product labeling. However, while these seals of approval might look great on a label, they do nothing to guarantee the product's safety and effectiveness.

RDAs/RDIs Taken Out of Context

The Food and Nutrition Board of the National Research Council, which is made up of experts from the U.S. and Canada, set the daily nutrient standards, called the Recommended Daily Allowances (RDA), which will not only exceed the daily needs but maintain a significant storage capacity of them.

The late Victor Herbert M.D. was professor of medicine and director, Nutrition Research Center at Mount Sinai School of Medicine. Dr. Herbert points out that another set of standards set by the World Health Organization (WHO), through its expert committee from a broader base internationally sets the Recommended Daily Intakes (RDI). Dr. Herbert states, "The RDIs tend to be lower than the RDAs because WHO does not believe *reserve stores need to be as high [my emphasis]*, as are traditional in the U.S." (*Total Nutrition: The Only Guide You'll Ever Need*. St. Martin Griffin, pp. 95–96, 1995).

Dr. Herbert further rightfully points out that "The RDA's provide a guide for dieticians and other health professionals for planning and evaluating diets for specific population groups, such as hospital patients, pregnant women, school children, and so forth. *They are not intended for specific individuals*" [my emphasis].

The major point here is that the RDAs or the RDIs are not a daily requirement and they "Allow far more than the average person needs" (Dr. Herbert).

Most consumers believe that they must consume a specified level of each nutrient each day to maintain adequate nutrient status and health—those "recommended daily allowances" we all see on product packaging. This is a fallacy. In fact according to Alfred Harper, PhD, Professor of Nutritional Sciences Emeritus at the University of Wisconsin, the recommended daily intakes "for essential nutrients are not average requirements. They exceed the needs of most, if not all, individuals in the specified group, specified by age and sex." Dr. Harper also states that the RDIs, "are standards for nutrient intakes for use by health professionals, not recommendations for the public" (*Modern Nutrition in Health and Disease*, 8th edition, 1,475–1,489). Dr. Harper has used vitamin C as an example of how the recommended daily intakes greatly exceeds our actual daily needs. While the recommendations for men would be to consume 60 milligrams or more of vitamin C per day, Dr. Harper contends that an intake of 30 mg per day is ample for an adult who is consuming fresh foods regularly. The reasoning for this is explained in detail in Chapter 3.

Similarly, the late Dr. Max Horwitt of the St. Louis University School of Medicine published a critique in 2001 of the Food and Nutrition Boards (FNB) of the Institute of Medicine's daily recommendation for vitamin E intake. Dr. Horwitt, who had been a member of three RDA committees and was involved in vitamin E research for over sixty-five years, commented that the FNB's 1989 decision to increase the recommended daily intake of vitamin E from 10 to 15 milligrams per day "benefits only the commercial interests involved in the sale of vitamin E" (*American Journal of Clinical Nutrition*, 2001; 73: 1003–5).

Lastly, consider the information provided by Judith Turnlund PhD, USDA-ARS Western Human Nutrition Research Center, Davis, California when referring to the current healthy upper limits for copper intake. "Research is suggesting that today's upper limit for American adults—set at 10 milligrams a day—may need to be lowered. Work is under way to see how the body handles excess copper. Already, an analysis of blood, urine, and other samples from nine healthy male volunteers aged 27 to 48 has shown a potentially unhealthy accumulation of copper after 4½ months of consuming 7.8 mg daily. It lowered one standard measure of the volunteers' antioxidant levels and also interfered with some immune system defenses. Though excretion of copper increased on this high-copper regimen, it wasn't enough to remove the excess." (*Agricultural Research Science Magazine*, January 2006, pg. 23).

Erroneous Assertions

Along with the deceptive marketing techniques outlined above, supplement manufacturers and their proponents perpetuate a plethora of myths and falsehoods meant to convince hapless consumers that they can't have a healthy diet without supplements. Be wary of any manufacturer or product that makes one of the following assertions.

"OUR SOILS ARE DEPLETED."

U.S. agribusiness has the enormous task of feeding not only millions of Americans but also millions of consumers all over the world. To do this requires an exceptional amount of care, science, and technology to make sure that the soil is properly managed. Part of this management process includes testing and fertilization when necessary to be sure the soil has adequate minerals not only to grow a particular crop, but to obtain adequate yields per acre and quality of produce. Plants require minerals for a variety of essential biological and physiological functions; if adequate minerals were unavailable as this myth purports, there would be a very noticeable—and likely, unacceptable to most consumers—change in the physical structure of both the plant and the produce.

"IT IS IMPOSSIBLE TO EAT RIGHT."

Even if this were true, chronic poor food choices *even with supplements* would leave you deficient in the thousands of plant compounds (phytochemicals) essential to good health. Due to advances in agricultural technology, food packaging, freezing, transportation and shipping, storage, etc. there has never been a time in history where the average consumer has had the luxury we now have in choosing from such a wide variety of quality nutrient dense foods which are available year-round. This issue is not "it is impossible to eat right," the issue is poor consumer decisions and lifestyle habits. Poor personal accountability for your own health will not be resolved by any supplement.

Just how many varieties of fresh fruits and vegetables, grains, etc. would someone have to have before they think they have enough options? Chapter 3 discusses this issue in detail.

"IT IS IMPOSSIBLE TO OBTAIN WHAT YOU NEED FROM FOOD ALONE."

I have already discussed the fallacy of attempting to apply the RDAs or RDIs literally to each consumer on a daily basis. That is not the intention of these guidelines as discussed. However, the supplement industry will attempt to misapply studies, which indicate that a large part of the population do not consume their daily intakes of these recommendations. So what? The three mechanisms discussed in Chapter 3—the storage capacity of all nutrients, the increased absorption rates in times of increased need; and the changes in retention rates in times of increased need, allow us to have a wide varied day to day intake and still maintain nutrient balance.

"MODERN FOOD PROCESSING DESTROYS MOST NUTRIENTS."

It is true that some of the methods used to process our food can destroy some nutrients. However, modern food processing actually increases the availability of nutrients in general to the vast majority of Americans by preventing spoilage, mold growth, and rancidity and extending storage time. Millions of Americans live in locations where fresh fruit and vegetables would be very difficult to obtain on a year-round basis. Modern food processing provides most consumers with a wide variety of high-quality foods twelve months of the year—and the payoff is an increase in availability of nutrients overall.

"MODERN STRESS INCREASES YOUR NUTRIENT NEEDS."

Stress is not a new phenomenon, and stress alone does not increase your nutrient needs. Much of our stress today is self-imposed and based on our wants, not our needs. In fact, the limited physical activity required for most lifestyles today has reduced our total caloric, and nutrient, need.

"MOST DISEASES ARE DIRECTLY ATTRIBUTED TO NUTRIENT DEFICIENCIES."

To the contrary, most diseases are attributed to viral, bacterial, or genetic causes, lifestyle choices, or the aging process. While a variety of diseases can be related to various nutrient deficiencies, they are minor in number compared to these other causes. Nutrient excesses from fat, carbohydrates, and protein has a far more direct negative impact on our health than any deficiencies.

"THIS PRODUCT BOOSTS YOUR IMMUNE SYSTEM."

This issue is discussed in detail in Chapter 4. In short, most consumers seem to believe that their immune system is something they want to have "boosted" or "stimulated," when in fact there is no physiological need for this. The body's immune system combats viral, fungal, and bacterial infections. If these infections are not present and your immune system is stimulated, what will it work to combat? Some researchers believe that the overstimulation of the immune system can lead to autoimmune diseases such as rheumatoid arthritis, diabetes, lupus, and multiple sclerosis. Keep in mind that through the body's natural adaptation to increased physical activity, athletes and active individuals already have an enhanced immune system.

Supplements on Trial: Lawsuits, Settlements, and Regulation in the Supplement Industry

In March 2002 Jerry Attaway, then physical development coordinator for the San Francisco 49ers, asked me to review a supplement manufacturer's claims for several products. As I studied the company's Web pages, I found its promotional statements fascinating. The manufacturer provided the typical misinformation about mineral-deficient soils resulting in mineral-deficient foods. But it went on to boldly proclaim itself "a product-based company first and a marketing company second. Why? Because we understand that it makes no difference how revolutionary or lucrative our marketing plan may be if our products do not work" (Ionyx International Inc.).

In fact, a more accurate statement from the sport supplement industry would be: "Deceptive marketing is the heart and soul of our industry. Why? Because we understand that it makes no difference how revolutionary we claim our products to be, consumers do not need them. So, without a lucrative and deceptive marketing plan, people would simply never buy our products."

In 2001, Consumers Union published a review of their findings regarding the sports supplement marketplace. In this review it stated, "People who take these products are actually conducting what amounts to a vast, uncontrolled clinical experiment on themselves with untested, largely unregulated medications" (Consumers Union Press Release, May 14, 2001). In a separate report by *Intelihealth Health News*, Nancy Metcalf, Senior Editor at *Consumer Reports* and the author of that magazine's review of sports supplements was quoted as saying, "I was stunned at how vigorously these products had been marketed based on little or no good scientific information" (*Intelihealth*, May 16, 2001, "Consumer Group Says Stay Away From Sports Supplements") (http://www.intelihealth.com/IH/ihtIH/WSIHW000/333/8015/321590.html).

The same report noted that David Rosenthal, head of Harvard University Health Services, agreed with *Consumer Reports*'s assessment of the supplement industry, urging that it be "heeded by coaches, parents and athletes." Rosenthal also stated, "It's time for us to say 'No.' . . . These things are not regulated, they are very erratic in their content from one batch to another . . . and they could perhaps be causing great danger." Parents must also remember that even the products, which have been tested, have only been tested on adults and not minors, which make up a significant portion of users.

Indeed, except for those supplements that claim to work like a drug, such as to treat, prevent, or cure a disease, the supplement industry is not subject to the rigorous regulations of the Food and Drug Administration (FDA). Vague claims go unchallenged and no advanced testing of safety or efficacy is required. Simply dump a hodgepodge mix of ingredients together, give it a name and market it. The Federal Trade Commission (FTC), the overseeing body for the supplement industry, does regularly challenge manufacturers' claims, but identifying and pursuing wrongdoers can take years. When the FTC does rule against a manufacturer, its typical recourse is to issue a cease-and-desist order. In other words, a simple written order to discontinue the false advertising with no significant financial repercussions. The FTC will levy fines after a company violates the cease-and-desist order. Initially, fines tend to be about $10,000 per violation; in some cases, fines are substantially higher, but considering a manufacturer's potential profits when deceiving consumers, these fines tend not to be a significant deterrent. Many companies appear to consider FTC fines simply a cost of doing business.

In 1994 Congress made it considerably easier for the supplement industry to deceive and swindle consumers when it passed the Dietary Supplement Health and Education Act (DSHEA). Thanks to this legislation, dietary ingredients used in dietary supplements are no longer subject to premarket safety evaluations—allowing manufacturers the legal latitude to market just about anything their labs can design, regardless of a lack of safety or effectiveness studies. Dr. Stephen Barrett, a nationally renowned consumer advocate and founder of Quackwatch, stated that the DSHEA "opened the flood gates to false claims for dietary supplements" (*Consumer Health Digest*, #01–32, 8/6/01). According to Dr. Barrett, passage of DSHEA "was spearheaded by a massive lobbying campaign organized by the marketers of dietary supplements and herbs. Although claimed to increase consumer protection, DSHEA's real purpose was to cripple FDA regulation of these products" (*Consumer Health Digest*, #02-46, 11/12/02). However, on April

1, 2004, "The Institute of Medicine, a nonprofit arm of the National Academy of Sciences, announced its decision that the FDA could now pull a product off the market based on data from animal studies, test-tube studies, and even based on similar products. The report also states, "given that supplements are assumed, rather than proven, to be safe before they are marketed, FDA does not need direct evidence of harm to humans to take actions." Also, "Changes in how an ingredient is formulated or processed raise the potential for new adverse effects" (www.nationalacadamies.org). While this was a positive step, supplement manufacturers still have far too little oversight. Simply put, DSHEA legislation has allowed the production and marketing of thousands of worthless products.

Of course, many companies that claim their products enhance health or athletic performance do not want to be regulated. They promote the notion that consumers should be allowed to decide for themselves whether a product is effective, with no oversight by the federal government. Yet few U.S. consumers would even consider purchasing unregulated foods or untested drugs, and they are beginning to demand the same kind of protection when it comes to supplements.

On a federal level even some legislators are turning their attention to the supplement industry. Senators have introduced two bills, S 1538 and S 722, that may, if ever passed, strengthen the FDA's ability to regulate this industry's marketing practices and to provide better protection of consumers (*Consumer Health Digest*, #03 -34, 8/26/03). S 1538 would increase funding for the FDA to regulate dietary supplements. As of January 2, 2006, the status of S 1583 was referred to the Senate committee on health, education, labor, and pensions. No further action has occurred.

S 722, the Dietary Supplement Safety Act of 2003, would require manufacturers of dietary supplements to submit to the FDA reports on adverse reactions. *The Consumer Health Digest* provided a summary of how this bill would affect manufacturers of supplements:

- Require the reporting of adverse effects.
- Enable the secretary of Health and Human Services (HHS) to conduct safety reviews and approve or disapprove continued marketing of suspect products.
- Require premarket approval of 'stimulant supplements,' products that speed metabolism, increase heart rate, constrict blood vessels, or cause the body to release adrenaline.
- Remove products that promote muscle growth or are advertised to promote muscle growth from the definition of 'dietary supplement,' which means that they have more stringent requirements to market.
- Eliminate the provision that would require the FDA to bear the burden of proof to show a supplement or ingredient in a supplement is unsafe.

In recent years, the supplement industry's blatant disregard for the truth has resulted in several major FTC and FDA settlements. One of the most significant recent actions taken against the sport supplement industry was the FDA's prohibiting of the sale of ephedra-containing supplements in 2003 due to ephedra's "unreasonable risk of illness or injury" (*FDA Consumer Alert*, 12/03). According to the FDA's report, ephedra has been "conclusively linked to significant adverse health outcomes, including heart ailments and strokes." Actions by consumer groups and investigative journalists have also shed light on the industry's deceptive practices. The lawsuits and other examples described here will make consumers more aware—and wary—of supplement makers' claims

FTC Settlements

The following consent agreements between manufacturers and the FTC are for settlement purposes only and they do not require or constitute an admission of a law violation according to the FTC.

The Federal Trade Commission settled with the Weider Corporation in 1984 for making false and misleading claims about its Anabolic Mega-Pak and Dynamic Life Essence products. Weider Corporation had failed to substantiate its claim that users would increase their muscular development more than nonusers, and in a shorter period. The FTC settlement cost Weider only $400,000. The products continued to be offered for sale, with the following disclaimer on the packaging: "As with all supplements, use of this product will not promote faster or greater muscle gains." (http://www.ftc.gov/opa/predawn/f85/weider2.htm)

In October 2000 the FTC released a press release entitled "Weider Nutrition Agrees to Settle FTC Charges of Unsubstantiated Claims for Herbal Dietary Supplements" and "would be required to pay $400,000 to the FTC for consumer redress" (http://www.ftc.gov/os/caselist/c3983.htm). In the FTC's Analysis of Proposed Consent Order, it states, "This matter involves advertisements for a dietary supplement called PhenCal or PhenCal 106. Advertisements claimed that PhenCal and PhenCal 106 have been proven to cause weight loss and to prevent the regaining of lost weight. These advertisements appeared in major newspapers such as the *New York Times*, the *Washington Post*, and *USA Today*.

"The proposed complaint alleges that Weider could not substantiate claims that PhenCal and PhenCal 106: (1) cause significant weight loss; (2) significantly increase a person's ability to maintain a reduced caloric diet and exercise program; (3) significantly reduce food cravings and eating binges; (4) prevent the regaining of lost weight; (5) are as effective as the prescription weight loss treatment commonly known as 'Phen-Fen'; and (6) are safe when used to promote or maintain weight loss. The complaint also alleges that Weider made false representation that claims (1), (3), (4), (5), and (6) above, had been scientifically proven" (http://www.ftc.gov/os/2000/10/weiderana.htm).

Great Earth International settled a case on January 4, 1988 after the FTC said the company "falsely claimed that three of its food supplements [including L-ornithine and L-arginine] would enable users to lose weight, build muscle, or promote healing."

The FTC settlement on February 13, 1989 required General Nutrition Corp (GNC), the largest retailer of nutritional supplements, to "pay a total of $600,000 for research and prohibited GNC from making false and unsubstantiated claims about its products," such as that they reduce the risk of cancer, promote weight loss or muscle growth, or retard aging. This particular order required the settlement funds to be divided "equally among the American Diabetes Association, the American Cancer Society, and the American Heart Association. One of the four FTC commissioners voting dissented from the agreement, "because the order leaves GNC free to sell products that it knows are deceptively labeled." She could not have been more astute. This commissioner clearly recognized that the industry views such settlements merely as a business expense.

On April 28, 1994 GNC agreed to pay $2.4 million in civil penalties to settle charges it had violated two previous FTC orders brought against them in 1969 and 1989 (*FTC News Notes*, April 25, 1994). This is the largest settlement to date but I do not believe at this time that it will deter most manufacturers. The FTC charged that GNC had made false claims for muscle building, weight loss, and human-growth-hormone release for products containing certain free amino acids and endurance enhancing claims. The case involved more than forty GNC products, including Dynamic Fat Burners, Fat Burners, Super Fat Burners, Super Fat Blocker, Fat Mobilizer Diet, Primary Tablet, Diet Pep, Protabalase ME, Cybergenics Phase I, Liquid Power Energy Lift, Muscle Fire Power, Hot Stuff, Cybergain, and Ginsana.

L&S Research Corporation agreed to pay $1.45 million in 1994 to settle deceptive advertising charges (*FTC News*, July 14,1994) for false and unsubstantiated claims of either increased muscle mass or weight loss due to use of its products sold under the name Cybergenics, which had been one of the more popular products among high school male athletes.

Body Wise International, Inc., agreed to settle FTC charges in 1995 that it made deceptive weight loss and cholesterol reduction claims for its products (*FTC News Notes*, June 6, 1995). FTC also charged "Body Wise with failing to disclose that healthcare professionals and others who gave testimonials for the products also were product distributors."

Also in 1995, Nature's Bounty and its subsidiaries Vitamin World, Inc., and Puritan's Pride, Inc., settled with the FTC for false advertising related to twenty-six supplements, including Sleeper's Diet, L-arginine, L-orthinine, octacosanol, and Ginsana. However, the company was fined only $250,000 (*FTC News Notes*, April 27, 1995).

On November 7, 1996 the FTC released settlement charges against several California companies charged with making the false claim that "most American diets lack adequate chromium and risk potentially serious health problems." These manufacturers claimed that chromium picolinate supplements burn fat, cause weight loss, increase muscle mass, reduce serum cholesterol, regulate blood sugar levels, and treat or prevent diabetes. According to the FTC complaint, "The companies failed to provide adequate substantiation for their claims." There were no financial repercussions levied against these companies stated in the settlement.

The companies involved in this settlement were Nutrition 21, "the sole supplier of chromium picolinate in the U.S.", Selene Systems, Inc., Victoria Bie, "doing business as Body Gold," and Universal Merchants, Inc. who according to the FTC marketed "through an infomercial starring Susan Ruttan, an actress who appeared in the long-running series *L.A. Law*, and in print ads in nutritional magazines." (http://www.ftc.gov/opa/1996/11/nut-21.htm).

The FTC reached a settlement with Met-Rx USA, Inc., and AST Nutritional Concepts, two manufacturers of androstenedione-related products, in November 1999. According to an FTC press release dated November 16, 1999, the settlement involved the "unsupported safety claims made in the marketing" of androstenedione products, as well as products containing the stimulants ephedrine and caffeine. The complaints also alleged "that the defendants claimed their androgen supplements, taken in the recommended doses, are safe, produce no or minimal negative side effects, and do not pose health or safety risks. The FTC alleges that the defendants lacked scientific evidence to support those claims." The FTC press release quoted several experts involved in the case, including General Barry McCaffrey, director of the Office of National Drug Control Policy, who stated, "Parents, coaches and athletes need to be aware of the real risks these substances pose for the lives and health of young people and athletes at all levels." In the complaint for permanent injunction and other equitable relief against Met-RX USA, Inc., under the consumer injury section on page 4 the FTC made the following strong statement: "As a result of defendant's unlawful acts or practices, consumers throughout the United States have suffered and continue to suffer risk of injury. Absent injunctive relief by this Court, the defendants are likely to continue to injure consumers and harm the public interest" (http://www.ftc.gov/os/1999/11/met-rxcmp.htm). These supplements were just as likely to increase estrogen levels as they would have testosterone. Several cancers are estrogen sensitive. They grow when exposed to estrogen.

The FTC levied one of the supplement industry's largest settlement fees on March 11, 2003, when it reported that Rexall Sundown would have to pay up to $12 million to settle charges regarding a purported cellulite treatment product. Rexall Sundown had falsely claimed that its product Cellasene, with sales of $40 million, would eliminate or substantially reduce fat. Rexall had also falsely claimed that "it had clinical evidence establishing Cellasene's efficacy." (http://www.ftc.gov/opa/2003/03/rexall.htm)

Nu Skin International and the U.S. Olympic Committee

On August 6, 1997, the FTC announced in a press release that the corporation Nu Skin International, of Provo, Utah, had agreed to pay $1.5 million in civil penalties "to settle FTC charges over the fat loss, muscle maintenance, and other claims it made for supplements containing chromium picolinate and L-carnitine." Nu Skin had been unable to "produce adequate substantiation" for its claims about the products Metabotrim, Overdrive, Glycobar, Appear Lite, and Breakbar.

In 2000 and 2002, the *American Journal of Clinical Nutrition* and the *International Journal of Sport Nutrition and Exercise Metabolism*, both peer-reviewed journals, further demonstrated the ineffectiveness of chromium supplements for muscle development or fat loss.

Despite the 1997 settlement and the ongoing negative assessments of chromium picolinate supplements, the *New York Times* has reported that "the [U.S. Olympic Committee] and Salt Lake organizers signed a deal through 2004 valued at $20 million with Nu Skin to supply Olympic training centers with supplements" (Selena Roberts, *New York Times*, January 20, 2002). It was an appalling move on the part of the USOC, which as early as 1995 had access to the results of preliminary animal studies conducted at Dartmouth College identifying chromium picolinate as a potentially harmful chemical that needed further evaluation. In 1999 University of Alabama researcher John B. Vincent, PhD, presented data at the American Chemical Society suggesting that chromium picolinate may damage DNA. According to Vincent, his research indicated "that care should be taken in the use of chromium picolinate. Careful investigation into the effects of long-term diet supplementation with chromium picolinate is needed to evaluate its mutagenic and carcinogenic potentials." What's more, a search of the literature would have turned up three studies published in 1977 about the relative toxicity of picolinic acid and its interference with normal iron metabolism (*Cancer Research*, Vol. 37; *Experimental and Molecular*

Pathology, Vol. 29; *Biochemical and Biophysical Research Communications,* Vol. 78). In 2003, Dr. Vincent again published warnings regarding the potential toxicity of chromium picolinate in the journal *Sports Medicine.* He states, "over a decade of human studies with chromium picolinate indicate that the supplement has not demonstrated effects on the body composition of healthy individuals, even when taken in combination with an exercise training program. Recent cell culture and rat studies have indicated that chromium picolinate probably generates oxidative damage of DNA and lipids and is mutagenic, althought the significance of these results on humans taking the supplements for prolonged periods of time is unknown and should be a focus for future investigations" (*Sports Medicine,* Vol. 33, No. 3, 2003, pp. 213–230 (18)). As noted in Chapter 1 with regard to endorsements, I believe the USOC should be much more conservative—and responsible—when considering whether to allow companies to use the Olympic Rings to promote their products. The FTC Web page provides well over a hundred cases of settlements against weight loss and health benefit products.

In 1998 the FTC published "Dietary Supplements: An Advertising Guide for Industry," through its Bureau of Consumer Protection. The purpose of this guide was to help ensure that "all parties who participate directly or indirectly, in the marketing of dietary supplements have an obligation to make sure that claims are presented truthfully and to check the adequacy and support behind those claims." As has already been illustrated, this is a very naïve effort by whoever authorized this report to control an industry who has demonstrated nothing but contempt for truth in marketing and advertising and the FTC.

FDA Settlements

The United Sates Attorney's Office, Central District of California, announced on October 3, 2003 that the Utah-based corporation Neways, Inc. pleaded guilty to the illegal sale of human growth hormone (HGH) throughout the United States. Neways has agreed to pay a criminal fine of $500,000 and to forfeit $1.25 million, "which represents profits the company made on the sale of Bio-Gevity from March 1999 until 2000." The sale of HGH is illegal without a physician's prescription and was distributed "through a network of independent distributors." According to the press release, approximately 100,000 bottles were sold. When HGH is in excess supply in the body it will cause a condition known as acromegaly, "which may include enlargement and distortion of facial features, hands and/or feet, skull, heart, and internal organs." Nerve function disorders, diabetes, and heart disease is also directly associated with HGH. (http://www.usdoj.gov/usao/cac/pr2003/137a.html)

Any product containing a substance defined as a drug is subject to the regulation and oversight of the FDA. On November 21, 2000, the FDA Talk Paper warned consumers against consuming any dietary supplement containing tiratricol, also known as TRIAC, a potent thyroid hormone popular among bodybuilders and weightlifters "that may cause serious health consequences including heart attacks and strokes." In 2003 the *International Journal of Sport Nutrition and Exercise Metabolism* reported that a tiratricol-containing weight loss product had caused hypothyroidism (inactivity of the thyroid gland) in "two physically fit adults," aged thirty-nine and forty. Ironically, the product was marketed as a metabolic accelerator and "fat burner," yet both subjects complained of lethargy and muscle weakness with a loss of appetite. After discontinuing use of the supplement, one subject's thyroid level returned to normal after forty days; the other subject's took five months to return to normal levels (*International Journal of Sport Nutrition and Exercise Metabolism*, 13 (1) 2003).

Parents really need to understand a point made by the FDA in this report. "Distribution of these products has been primarily through retail sales to health food stores, fitness centers, and gymnasiums." Although recalled, this is another example of the renegade attitude of many in the sports and general supplement industry.

In another example of FDA intervention, in February 2003 the FDA's director of the Center for Food Safety and Applied Nutrition, sent official warning letters to American Bodybuilding (a subsidiary of Optimum Nutrition, Inc.,) and AST Sports Science. These supplement makers had been claiming that their ephedrine- and androstenedione-containing products would help build muscle. The FDA found that several of the claims violated the federal rules governing unsubstantiated claims regarding changes in either the structure or function of the body.

On April 30, 2003, the FDA ordered Nature's Youth to destroy $515,000 worth of a product the company had claimed would "enhance the body's natural production of Human Growth Factors" and would "improve physical performance, speed recovery from training, increase cardiac output, and increase immune functions." Although Nature's Youth attempted to justify its claims by a misapplication of an article published in the *New England Journal of Medicine* in 1990 (Vol. 323:1–6, No. 1, July 5, 1990), the FDA determined that the claims were unsubstantiated. The *New England Journal of Medicine* report had been so widely misrepresented by the sport supplement industry that the journal issued the following statement: "If people are induced to buy a human growth hormone releaser on the basis of research published in the *Journal* they are being misled" (*New England Journal of Medicine,* Vol. 348: 777–778, No. 9, February 27, 2003).

Consumer Group Reports

In 1992 the National Council Against Health Fraud published its findings on deceptive claims in the supplement industry in the *National Strength and Conditioning Association Journal.* A similar report prepared by the New York Department of Consumer Affairs followed soon after. The NYDCA's report stated that 56 percent of full-page advertisements for nutritional supplements in four popular bodybuilding magazines were worthless and possible harmful, citing Champion Nutrition's product Metabolol, Twin Labs' Amino Fuel 2000, and Weider Food Supplements' Dynamic Fat Burners in particular. The NYDCA vowed to begin curbing the deception and exploitation of susceptible individuals by issuing "notices of violation" of the New York consumer protection law.

Since 1997 the American Council on Science and Health, one of the most well-respected consumer advocacy groups in the U.S., has called for the "regulation of all ephedra-containing supplements as over-the-counter drugs" instead of masquerading as over-the-counter supplements. ("Imitation of Ecstasy: A Commentary on Ephedra Products," April 1, 1997)

Media Reports on Met-Rx

Increasingly, investigative journalists are serving as watchdogs over the supplement industry. An *NBC Dateline* broadcast on October 6, 1996, entitled "Hype in a Bottle" investigated Met-Rx USA, Inc., a maker of sports supplements. The *Dateline NBC* report revealed that Met-Rx had failed to provide published peer-reviewed documentation to substantiate its advertising claims of enhancing muscular development, relying instead on the placebo effect, testimonials, or natural improvements to support its claims.

I first contacted Met-Rx in 1995 because of a request made to the National Council Against Health Fraud for an opinion on the product claims. As the ergogenic aid coordinator for the NCAHF, this was my responsibility. I contacted Met-Rx to request data supporting its claims for its products. One item I received was an unpublished "Met-Rx Substantiation Report" dated October 1993 that associated the product with the well-respected Cooper Clinic in Dallas, Texas. The report noted that several Dallas Cowboys had gained an average of 2.5 to 3 pounds of lean body mass weekly for six weeks when using a Met-Rx product—an obvious red flag. I knew that unless the athletes had been utilizing large quantities of steroids, these results would be impossible. I contacted the Cooper Clinic, making them aware of the possible misrepresentation, and later received a copy of a letter sent to Met-Rx from the Cooper Clinic president and medical director. The letter stated, in part, "It has come to my attention that you are using the Cooper Clinic name without permission with misleading information and are otherwise engaging in unfair competition by featuring our name. If you continue to engage in the unauthorized use of our name, consumers are likely to erroneously believe that Met-Rx is in some way approved, endorsed, licensed or otherwise associated with the Cooper Clinic. Such an erroneous impression will inevitably dilute the goodwill and value of our name, attributable to the Cooper Clinic and damage to our interests and reputation. In view of the foregoing, I request that you immediately cease and desist your unauthorized use of the Cooper Clinic name."

In February 1995, the Penn State *Sports Medicine Newsletter* (3; 6) published a report titled "Is It Real or Is It Met-Rx?" that concluded, "Met-Rx is a popular, expensive nutritional mix. Its claims of fat loss and increased muscle mass have not been proven by scientifically accepted methods. Met-Rx instructions include a weight-training program, which, by itself, could very well lead to increased muscle mass and less body fat. *There is no listed ingredient that separates it from other products on the market* [my emphasis]. Until independent, objective and meticulously controlled studies are conducted that show significant physiological changes, do not expect any more from Met-Rx than from other formulated products."

More bad press for Met-Rx followed in Melvin Williams's 1997 book *The Ergogenics Edge: Pushing the Limits of Sports Performance.* Dr. Williams, a professor in the Department of Exercise Science, Physical Education, and Recreation at Old Dominion University, wrote, "There appear to be no scientific data specifically evaluating the effectiveness of Met-Rx. One study provided some indirect evidence indicating that Met-Rx is not an effective sports ergogenic." In the study Dr. Williams references, one group of individuals received the protein supplement Met-Rx and another study group did not; there were no significant differences between the two groups for body composition or strength changes.

In 1999 the *Journal of Exercise Physiology* online reported that there were no significant differences between Met-Rx and a carbohydrate supplement in changes in soft tissue lean mass (muscle tissue) or strength changes as measured by one repetition max bench press (*JEPonline*, 1999, 2 (2):24–39).

The Houston Texans Strength & Conditioning Program guide for their athletes, written by Dan Riley and Ray Wright helps their athletes make better dietary decisions through education. On page 5 of this guide Riley and Wright quote William J. Evans Ph.D., the director of the Noll Physiological Research Center at Penn State regarding Met-Rx. "I don't see anything magic in the ingredients. The protein contained in Met-Rx is milk based, which is the highest quality you can get. But you can get the same thing in milk by itself. If an athlete insists on using a protein supplement, we recommend non-fat powdered milk, which contains calcium and is a rich source of protein."

The FDA and Ephedra

Even though the FDA banned ephedrine-containing supplements in April 2004, I believe the following information is still important to further illustrate why this industry needs further legislation to regulate it. Some in the industry have already replaced ephedrine with the stimulant synephrine in some products, which is also known as bitter orange.

On October 28, 2003 John M. Taylor, Associate Commissioner for Regulatory Affairs with the FDA testified before the Committee on Commerce United States Senate during a hearing on dietary supplements. Some of the points Mr. Taylor made relating to the athletic marketplace and ephedra are provided (http://www.fda.gov/ola/2003/dietarysupplements1028.html):

- A recent study by RAND concluded that ephedra has minimal if any proven benefit for enhancing sports performance.
- Ephedra acts like an adrenaline boost, stressing the heart, raising blood pressure, and increasing metabolism.
- The stimulating effects of ephedra may mask the signs of fatigue, causing even the most well-conditioned athletes to push beyond their physical limits. Thus, ephedra's risks are potentially much more serious for competitive athletes than for the general population.
- Ephedra should not be used by people who engage in strenuous activity.
- On Febuary 28, 2003 the FDA warned 26 firms to cease making unproven claims that ephedra-containing dietary supplements enhance athletic performance based upon the misinformation provided on their Web sites.
- On February 6, 2004 the FDA began prohibiting the sale of dietary supplements containing ephedra alkoloids. (FDA News 2/6/04)

With regard to the stimulatory effects of ephedra and athletes, I will provide one brief personal illustration, which supports Mr. Taylor's points as to why athletes or active consumers should have been the last group to consider taking these products. On August 8, 2000 at approximately 8:30 am, I was beginning a preemployment strength-screening test on a twenty-three-year-old well-developed male body-builder, 5'9" and 223 pounds. The test involved the applicant having to demonstrate the capability to safely lift the required heavy loads for the particular oil-well servicing company. Prior to the test, the standard blood pressures and heart rates are taken in order to eliminate any applicant with excessive resting blood pressures or resting heart from the screening. This particular candidate appeared very nervous and agitated and was unable to explain why but only apologized for his inability to sit still. Due to his size and obvious strength, his agitated state was unrelated to what he would have been expected to lift. His resting heart rate was 110 bpm and his blood pressure was 280/120. I obviously would not allow him to continue and he volunteered that he had taken his usual sports supplement that morning because he intended to go to the gym to lift after the testing was completed. He stated he had taken the sports product Ripped Fuel, which contained ephedrine as well as caffeine at the time.

My point should be obvious. This otherwise young and healthy individual would have been a perfect candidate for a stroke or heart attack if he had proceeded to the gym to lift with a resting blood pressure as high as his was that morning. Keep in mind, he had no symptoms of headache or pain and other than the extreme nervousness, was unaware of what was taking place physiologically.

By 2004 the FDA was aware of at least 150 deaths associated with the use of ephedrine-based "nutritional supplements" (*Legal News Watch*, 8/25/04). However, this early figure was based upon the limited data the FDA had been able to obtain from the marketers of ephedrine products and did not fully represent the harm ephedrine products were causing.

A report, *Adverse Event Reports from Metabolife*, from the Special Investigations Division, Committee on Government Reform from the U.S. House of Representatives in 2002 makes the following statement in the Executive Summary. "The largest manufacturer of dietary supplements containing ephedra is Metabolife International, Inc. Prior to August 2002, Metabolife repeatedly informed the Food and Drug Administration that the company had 'never been made aware of any adverse health events by consumers of its products.' It also consistently maintained that its products are absolutely safe."

In fact, Metabolife ended up "giving the FDA copies of over 13,000 reports the company had received between 1997 and 2002 of adverse reactions to its products." Under the Key Findings section of this report, the following statements were made:

- The Metabolife records include nearly 2,000 reports of significant adverse reactions to Metabolife products. These include 3 deaths, 20 heart attacks, 24 strokes, 40 seizures, 465 episodes of chest pains, and 966 reports of heart rhythm disturbances. There were also hundreds of consumer complaints for high blood pressure and disturbing psychiatric symptoms such as anxiety, mood changes, or psychosis.
- The records indicate that many of the significant adverse events involve consumers who were young, in good health, and taking recommended dosages.
- Metabolife's handling of the adverse event reports exhibits indifference to the health of consumers.
- Metabolife's records contradict Metabolife's claims that it was unaware of consumer complaints of adverse health effects.

On July 22, 2004, the Department of Justice released a news release stating "that a Grand Jury sitting in the Southern District of California returned an eight-count indictment against Metabolife and its founder Michael J. Ellis." The indictment charged Metabolife with "making false, fictitious and fraudulent representations to the FDA and two counts of corruptly endeavoring to influence, obstruct and impede proceedings concerning the regulation of dietary supplements containing ephedra."

The news release also stated that Metabolife and Ellis were "charged with falsely representing a number of different material facts to the FDA in a letter dated April 17, 1998 and February 9, 1999. These representations included false statements by the defendants that 'Metabolife had never received one notice from a consumer that any serious adverse health event has occurred because of the ingestion of Metabolife 356' and that the company had a claims-free history."

Currently, Metabolife is in the midst of settling various lawsuits related to the serious health problems associated with the use of its products. The *San Diego Tribune* reported on June 24, 2004, that Metabolife or its insurers have paid at least $5 million to settle twenty-nine lawsuits and that more than 150 others are still pending.

Insurance policy writers who insure the companies who market ephedra products have begun to take notice of the increasing liability associated with these products. Consider the following comments from an article called "Herbalife, Other Ephedra Marketers Face Soaring Insurance Rates" by David Evans that appeared on the health industry watchdog Web site Quackwatch.org on April 11, 2002:

1. *Herbalife International Inc. continues to sell weight-loss products containing ephedra, following lawsuits blaming the substance for customer deaths, and six-fold increase in product liability insurance expense.*
2. *Robert Hartwig, chief economist for the Insurance Information Institute, said ephedra insurance premiums have increased along with adverse incidence reports and lawsuits. "You have a situation where the house is on fire," said Hartwig. "If your house was already on fire, it is very unlikely we would write a policy." More than a half dozen other public traded companies also continue to sell ephedra products, while unable to obtain desired levels of insurance.*
3. *Herbalife said in its federal filing that its product-liability insurance premium soared from $400,000 in 2000 to $2.5 million last year, even as its deductible increased 10-fold to $5 million, and its coverage limit fell by $10 million to $40 million.*

The FDA's 2004 ruling on ephedra-containing products represents a huge leap forward in protecting consumers from the supplement industry's deceptive practices. Perhaps more of these kinds of rulings, coupled with increasing fines, fees, and insurance costs—and the resulting impact on these companies' bottom lines—will persuade the manufacturers to change their business practices. Clearly, their consciences alone do not provide enough incentive.

The Dangers of Mislabeling

In 2004, Kicker Vencill, an Olympic-hopeful swimmer who had been banned from competition for four years as a result of testing positive for steroids, successfully sued Ultimate Nutrition of Farmington, Connecticut, for $578,635. The swimmer claimed that the multivitamins he was taking were contaminated with steroid precursors and was responsible for his positive steroid test (*USA Today*, 5/25/2005, "Banned swimmer wins case over supplements" by Ben Fox).

According to court documents, UCLA laboratory analysis of the multivitamin product Vencill took revealed that it was "contaminated by three anabolic agents, androstenediol, androstenedione, and norandrostenedione, in sufficient concentrations to have caused the positive doping results" (Court of Arbitration for Sport, pp. 7–9) or (www.tas-cas.org). The Court of Arbitration for Sport stated, on page 19 of their report "Kicker Vencill has definitely established that the Ultimate Nutrition Super Complete Capsules that he was taking on January 21, 2003 were contaminated with steroids."

However, according to some limited media reports, Ultimate Nutrition was able to get the Superior Court of the State of California in Orange County to vacate the earlier court decision in July of 2005. The report states that Ultimate Nutrition "hired the University of Southern California to test the product . . . and that all of the USC studies were negative for the alleged contaminants" (http://www.npicenter.com/anm/templates/newsATemp.aspx?articleid=13000&zoneid=2).

The May 28, 2001, *Consumer Health Digest* of the NCAHF reported that Senator Orrin Hatch was "being pressed to amend the DSHEA of 1994 because some of the Olympic athletes who were caught cheating with steroids last summer blamed mislabeled or adulterated dietary supplements made in Utah as the culprit." In 2003 Senator Hatch did secure $1 million to help remove illegal supplements from the marketplace. However, this will do little if anything to turn the tide of misinformation and false advertising, which the bill he coauthored, the DSHEA, started in the first place The supplement industry in general is heavily concentrated in Utah, the senator's home state. The same newsletter stated, "Enrico Castellacci, president of the Italian soccer doctors' association, warned that some nutritional supplements sold legally in Italy contain the banned steroid nandrolone." However, Don Catlin, MD, of the UCLA Olympic Analytical Laboratory in Los Angeles, has reported, "Trace contamination of androstenedione with 19-norandrostenedione is sufficient to cause urine tests results positive for 19-norandrosterone, the standard marker for nandrolone use" (*JAMA* 2000, 284; 2618–2621). It would initially appear, that the removal of androstenedione from the marketplace would have resolved this issue. However, the *Washington Post* "obtained five dietary supplements—each of which touted its ability to build muscle fast—available online and asked a prominent Los Angeles researcher to test them. Don Catlin, who directs the U.S. Olympic drug-testing lab at UCLA, said four of the products contained previously undetected anabolic steroids. One contained a steroid that came to the attention of authorities just two years ago but, until now, was thought to be in only limited circulation." He stated, "they are all going to be effective" (*Washington Post*, Tuesday, October 18, 2005 page E01 by Amy Shipley) or (http://www.washingtonpost.com/wp-dyn/content/article/2005/10/17/AR2005101701622.html)

The article also stated "two officials with prominent U.S. dietary supplement companies, who spoke on condition of anonymity, said it is easy for companies to outwit drug testers. There is an unlimited pool of steroids . . . you could do this for the next 100 years . . . the longer they do not pay attention the more rampant it gets."

Many seemingly innocuous vitamin supplement products are mislabeled, with serious consequences. The *New England Journal of Medicine* reported that a forty-two-year-old male experienced vitamin D intoxication after ingesting a vitamin D supplement. According to researchers, the vitamin D3 supplements contained "26 to 430 times the amount listed by the manufacturer." (Letter to the editor, 2001; 345 (1): 66).

On May 17, 2000, ConsumerLab.com reported on their results of tests run on twenty-six brands of vitamin C. The results indicated that "fifteen percent either did not contain the entire claimed ingredient or failed to breakdown as needed for absorption by the body. Unexpectedly, the results were no better for products claiming to meet USP [United States Pharmacopoeia] standards compared to products not making such a claim." A USP insignia on a supplement label is often cited, even by professionals, as reassurance that the product has met standards for purity, potency, disintegration, and dissolution. As this study demonstrates, it is not always the case.

The *Clinical Journal of Sports Medicine* reported on a study conducted at UCLA's Division of Sports Medicine in 2001 in which researchers analyzed twelve brands of over-the-counter purported anabolic-androgenic supplements (androstenedione-related products). They found that all twelve brands were mislabeled. The researchers stated, "One brand contained 10 mg testosterone, a controlled steroid, another contained 77% more than the label stated, and 11 of 12 contained less than the amount stated on the label." They concluded that "these mislabeling problems show that labels of the dietary steroid supplements studied herein cannot be trusted for content and purity information" (*Clin J Sport Med*, October 2001; 11 (4) 254–258).

An investigation by the International Olympic Committee doping laboratory in Cologne, Germany, reported that from "October 2000 until November 2001 634 non-hormonal nutritional supplements were obtained in 13 countries from 215 suppliers." The Institute of Biochemistry, where the supplements were analyzed, reported that "out of the 634 samples analyzed 94 (14.8%) contained prohormones not declared on the label" (*Olympic Coach*, Spring 2002, Vol. 12, #2).

Mislabeling of nutrition bars and similar products is a rampant problem: In October 2001 the independent testing lab Consumer Lab.com announced that eighteen of thirty (60 percent) of the nutrition bars it tested were improperly labeled.

Weider Nutrition Group, Inc., settled a nutrition bar–related class action suit in June 1998, in the Superior Court of California, County of Contra Costa (Case No. C96-05610). The complaint alleged that the nutritional information contained on the company's Steel Bar wrappers was inaccurate and that WNG had published false and misleading advertisements for the product. According to the attorneys for the plaintiffs, Farrow, Bramson, Baskin and Plutzik, LLP of Walnut Creek, California, introductory remarks on page 1 "WNG repeatedly lied about the nutritional content of its product. In a nutshell, WNG knowingly stated that the bars had less unhealthy content (fat and sodium) and more nutritional value (vitamins and minerals) than the product really had."

"WNG's own testing during the class period consistently showed that the bars had more bad ingredients and fewer good ingredients than promised on the labels. For example, in 1995 the coconut bars' labels advertised 4 grams of fat and 35 milligrams of sodium. Independent laboratory tests showed that the bars had more than 16 grams of fat and 235 milligrams of sodium—more than 4 times the stated amount of fat and more than 8 times the claimed amount of sodium. Furthermore, the label did not disclose that there was sucrose (table sugar) in the bars. At the same time, the labels touted fractionated canola oil, a 'healthy' fat as an ingredient, when in reality no bar ever contained a drop of it. Similarly, the amount of vitamins and minerals in the bars was significantly overstated on the labels. These deceptions rendered the Steel Bars worthless to their consumers."

Although WNG denied the material allegations, it agreed to pay a maximum of $75,000 to reimburse consumers who purchased Steel Bars between December 20, 1994, and April 24, 1998. It also agreed to donate $2 million of product to a southern California food bank and to pay attorney and court costs.

On May 9, 2001, Intelihealth Health News reported, "Metabolife International is recalling 1.5 million energy bars because they contain excessive levels of vitamin A." The bars were reported to contain "about 32,500 IUs of vitamin A," an extremely unsafe amount. In fact, this "energy" bar had enough vitamin A to potentially precipitate vitamin A overdose symptoms of fatigue, malaise, and lethargy; daily intake of this bar would have led to chronic toxicity that, according to the clinical nutrition text *Modern Nutrition in Health and Disease*, could result in "baldness, failure of muscular coordination, bone and muscle pain, inflammation affecting the lips and the delicate membranes that lines the eyelid, headache, liver poisoning, hyperlipidemia, enlargement of the bones, itching of various external sites, various skin disorders, and visual impairment" (*MNHD*, 8th edition, pg. 298). And for women, extended use of this product could have had adverse affects on the reproductive process and, for pregnant women, the fetus.

In 2006, attorney Douglas Brooks of Gilman and Pastor LLP in Boston, Massachusetts, filed a class-action lawsuit against Muscle Marketing USA, Inc., manufacturer of the liquid creatine supplement called Creatine Serum. According to Brooks, the label for the product at the time stated that it contained "pure creatine monohydrate." Product testing revealed that it only contained "trace amounts of creatine—less than 1% of the label claims," according to an e-mail from Brooks. The rest of the product was the ineffective waste-product creatinine.

Brooks also pointed out that the New Zealand Commerce Commission (their version of our FTC) also fined Muscle Marketing USA $75,000 (an obviously insignificant deterrent) "for breaking the Fair Trading Act" (*Communiqué issue 8*: December 2004). This report stated, "In sentencing, Judge Everett said that Muscle Marketing's claims about its product were so far from actual reality that it was a very bad case of a misleading statement. 'The company was highly culpable. On a scale of 1–10 it was an 8.'"

The report also stated that this is "another example of a product where consumers are utterly reliant on claims being made by the company because they have no realistic means of checking the actual composition or effectiveness of the product" (www.comcom.govt.nz/Publications/ContentFiles/Documents/COM11611_communique_DecO%5B2%5D.pdf).

The National Collegiate Athletic Association's Divisions II and III have made "weight-gain/muscle-building supplements a nonpermissible expense," according to *Training & Conditioning* magazine (1999:3). In August 2000 the *NCAA News* reported that Division I institutions had adopted a similar policy. In California, the organization that oversees the high school sports programs statewide, the California Interscholastic Federation (CIF), is in the process of adopting similar measures. Nonpermissible items include amino acids, protein powders, condroitin, creatine, ginseng, glucosamine, beta-hydroxy beta-methylbutyrate (HMB), and ephedrine-based or related central nervous system stimulant products. The NCAA continues to deem permissible vitamins and minerals, energy bars, calorie-replacement drinks (such as Ensure and Boost), and fluid and electrolyte-replacement drinks (such as Gatorade and Powerade). Most of these items have a legitimate place in athletics. However, male athletes should never consume a mineral supplement that contains iron unless prescribed by a physician. As long as the mislabeling of some of these items continues to be a problem, the NCAA should add vitamin and mineral supplements and some "energy" bars to its list of nonpermissible expenses.

Lastly, consumers who believe they benefit from any of the over-the-counter supplements can check for labeling accuracy for many of the products at ConsumerLab.com. Of interest, on March 15, 2005 the FTC dismissed a complaint from the Council of Responsible Nutrition, a trade group who represents dietary supplement distributors and manufacturers, that "alleges that ConsumerLab's 'entire business model represents an egregious form of consumer fraud and deception." ConsumerLab simply evaluates content validity of over-the-counter supplement products. Something, as the consumer now understands, would make this industry very nervous.

3 VITAMINS AND MINERALS

THE THREE NUTRIENT BALANCE MECHANISMS

As we've explored in Chapters 1 and 2, the supplement industry uses many methods to convince consumers that obtaining an exceptional level of physical development—or even maintaining a physically active lifestyle—is simply not possible without dietary supplements, even for individuals with good dietary habits. Here's what supplement manufacturers don't want you to know: with reasonable effort, it's actually quite easy to achieve nutrient balance, even when intense physical training or heavy labor are part of your daily activities.

Indeed, even a very active individual with some bad eating habits—for example, a rapidly physically maturing high school athlete whose regular diet is of marginal quality—can quickly learn to adjust his or her diet to obtain enough nutrients to support both muscular development and enhanced performance—*without* using dietary supplements.

The secret to nutrient balance lies in understanding three well-designed biological mechanisms, which through a complex system of checks and balances can help the human body maintain nutrient homeostasis (balance), even over a broad range of nutrient intakes. These mechanisms are:

- storage capacity of nutrients,
- changes in absorption rate of nutrients when needs increase, and
- retention of nutrients or changes in excretion rates of nutrients when needs increase.

Many people—including some health professionals—are unaware of the processes by which these three mechanisms help maintain physical health. This chapter will give you a clear understanding of how these mechanisms can help you maintain nutrient balance while consuming a wide range of nutrients, frequently well below what is recommended. An understanding of these mechanisms will arm you against the nagging claims of the supplement industry that a healthy diet, or even an infrequent marginal diet, alone is not enough to support an athletic lifestyle. Moreover, it will explain how it's possible for millions of people around the world who do not have access to the quantity and wide varieties of food enjoyed by developed countries to stay healthy.

Consider this fact. How do thousands of athletes who frequently consume only one half of what is recommended for many nutrients due to poor food choices, do not take supplements yet have been able to become extremely well-developed physically and highly skilled athletically?

Of course these three mechanisms are not without limitations, and they will not sustain nutrient balance in an individual who habitually makes poor food choices. Other plant chemicals found in fruits, vegetables, and whole grains are just as necessary as specific vitamins and minerals for health; bear in mind that poor food choices eliminate hundreds if not thousands of plant chemicals that are likely to play as vital a role in long-term health as the "major nutrients" discussed here.

As you consider these three mechanisms of nutritional balance, keep in mind a comment attributed to Benjamin Caballero, MD, a member of the National Academy of Sciences Food and Nutrition Board: "There has been a transition from focusing on minimum needs to the reality that today our problem is excess calories and, yes, excesses of vitamins and minerals as well." (*New York Times*, 5/2/2003, "Vitamins: More May Be Too Many," by Gina Kolata).

There are certainly circumstances where vitamin and mineral supplements are appropriate, which is discussed in the last chapter. However, the point of this chapter is to illustrate that even if you have several consecutive days of one half of the recommended intake of any nutrient the biological mechanisms discussed will maintain a balance.

Storage Capacity

There's a common misconception about vitamins and minerals, even among many professional educators, that we must consume a set dosage of these nutrients *every day*, or we will be deficient in that nutrient the next day. Nutrition experts say differently.

> *Expert Input*
>
> **Victor Herbert, MD, JD, professor of medicine at Mount Sinai School of Medicine and a Federation of American Societies for Experimental Biology (FASEB)-recognized expert in nutrition. From the book from the Mount Sinai School of Medicine *Total Nutrition: The Only Guide You'll Ever Need*. (St. Martin's Griffin 1995, pg. 99).**
>
> Contrary to popular belief, it is not necessary to consume water-soluble vitamins every single day: the body stores enough to provide reserves that last for a few weeks to months or even longer in some cases. It is important, however, that the average intake over a week or two provides the variety of foods that supply all the

> essential vitamins. The liver is the body's main nutrient storehouse. It absorbs and stores excess nutrients from the blood, and releases into the blood those nutrients that are not coming into the blood from the diet.

Consumers are told that to maintain optimal health and keep the maximum level of nutrient concentration in the body tissues, they need to consume supplements daily. There is no evidence that this is true. The tissue saturation point, or storage capacity, simply is the body's maximum retention of a given nutrient before that nutrient is excreted in the urine, is catabolized (broken down) to other products, or becomes toxic. The body can maintain a range of storage capacities of nutrients for a specific reason: so that physiological needs will still be met even when the quality or quantity of food intake diminishes. This storage capacity function is still essential in many countries with limited food availability or poor standards of living, but in the United States and other developed countries, the biological saturation point essentially comes into play only when an individual is ill for an extended period, weeks to months, or refuses to follow reasonable dietary practices. In North America today, the saturation point probably does more to protect us from the effects of excessive vitamin/mineral supplementation than to protect us in times of need. The point is this: there is a large buffer zone between *maximum* storage and the amount of a given nutrient that must be present in the body for proper cellular function and development. Some nutrients, like copper, have relatively little in storage compared to other trace elements. Still, this small amount of copper is significant when compared to the body's daily needs. An adult human contains only about 50 to 150 mg of copper (*Modern Nutrition in Health and Disease*, 8th edition, pg. 234, 1994 Lea & Febiger), but an adult's daily need for copper is only 2 to 3 mg. Thus, even when the amount of copper in storage does not appear to be significant, it is more than adequate for times of reduced copper availability or increased need.

Following are examples of the body's storage capacities for many nutrients, gathered from scientific journals, college textbooks and interviews with experts. Keep in mind as you read these examples that no one advocates or suggests that a low normal nutrient status may not put you at risk for potential adverse health effects. Low iron status is a good example of this point. The simple point is the inherent buffer of nutrient balance we all have to work with if we just make appropriate food choices most of the time.

VITAMIN C

A man of average size can have a total body pool of vitamin C as high as 1,500 mg. Consuming 60 mg/day of vitamin C can attain that level; with negligible intake it would take approximately sixty days for the amount in storage to decline to 300 mg. According to Alfred Harper, PhD, E.V. McCollum Professor of Nutritional Sciences Emeritus at the University of Wisconsin, an intake of "30 mg per day, an amount that would maintain a body pool of about 1000 mg and provide a reserve lasting 20 to 30 days, should be ample" (*MNHD,* 8th edition, pg. 1,480). Dr. Harper also stated that "differences in judgment on the size of the desirable reserve resulted in the FAO/WHO recommending 30 mg per day of ascorbic acid [vitamin C] as a safe intake for men, whereas the U.S. NRS/NAS recommends 60 mg per day or more, implying that saturation of tissues should be the criterion of adequacy and that individuals consuming between 30 and 60 mg daily are at risk for inadequate intakes, even though no evidence of the health benefit from the higher intake has been demonstrated" (*MNHD,* 8th edition, pg. 1,480). The most recent recommended dietary intake (RDI) for vitamin C is 90 mg per day (even though, again, the benefits of this high level are unproven). In another study, healthy male prisoners who consumed 75 mg of ascorbic acid per day were calculated to have pool sizes of 1,486 to 1,542 mg (*American Journal of Clinical Nutrition*, 1971; 24: 444–4).

How hard is it to maintain this level of vitamin C? Not hard at all. Following is a list of common foods and their vitamin C content, found in Bowes and Church's *Food Values of Portions Commonly Used*, 14th edition:

- cantaloupe, 1 cup = 68 mg
- one medium guava = 165 mg
- kiwi fruit = 75 mg
- one navel orange = 80 mg
- strawberries, 1 cup = 85 mg
- frozen peaches, 1 cup = 235 mg
- red raw chilies (3½ oz.) = 369 mg (if you can handle the heat)

In the early 1980s the Food and Nutrition Board of the National Research Council/National Academy of Sciences mentioned in Chapter 1 concluded that intakes of only 40 or 30 mg per day of vitamin C would provide a body pool of 900 mg/day, enough to protect against deficiency symptoms for at least one month for an average size man. Robert Jacobs, PhD, research chemist with the USDA Western Human Nutrition Research Center at the University of California, Davis, noted that "no signs of ascorbic acid deficiency have been shown at this pool size" and that "higher body reserves have not been shown to provide increased health benefit" (*MNHD*, 8th edition, pg. 443).

NIACIN

In 1997 three leading experts on niacin (Robert Russel, MD, professor of medicine and nutrition at Tufts University; Dr. Robert Jacobs of UC–Davis; and Elaine Jacobson, PhD, University of Kentucky Medical Center) responding to my faxed inquiry concurred that even with a diet containing only one-third of the recommended daily allowance of niacin (14 mg for women and 16 mg for men), the body's storage capacity for niacin would last three to six weeks or longer.

RIBOFLAVIN

The recommended intake for riboflavin is 1.1 to 1.3 mg/day and according to Donald McCormick, PhD, professor and chairman of the Department of Biochemistry at Emory School of Medicine, a recognized expert in riboflavin metabolism, if an individual's diet provided no riboflavin, "it would take several weeks to months to lead to severe depletion/deficiency." (faxed communication 2/11/97).

Of course, no diet has a zero intake of riboflavin, but consuming one-half of the recommended daily intake is common. The point is that a natural "buffer zone" comes into play when appropriate foods are not available or needs have temporarily increased (for example, with increased physical activity).

PANTOTHENIC ACID

No recommended intake for pantothenic acid has been established, only adequate intake, which is 5 mg/day for adult males and females. According to a review of pantothenic acid in the *Journal of Nutrition and Biochemistry*, "[P]antothenic deficiency has been induced in humans in 4 to 9 weeks by use of a pantothenate-deficient diet supplemented with omega-methyl pantothenate, a metabolic antagonist" (*J Nutr Biochem* 1996; 7:313). This simply means that it took four to nine weeks to produce a pantothenic acid deficiency in healthy adults who were ingesting a completely deficient pantothenic acid diet. This does not reflect the margin of safety, which would be substantially longer, that would occur in someone ingesting one-half of optimal intake.

PYRIDOXINE (VITAMIN B-6)

Stephen Coburn, PhD, a Federation of American Societies for Experimental Biology (FASEB) recognized expert on pyridoxine with the Department of Biochemistry, Fort Wayne State Development Center, faxed to my office on 2/17/97 the following comment: "With an intake of .5 mg/day or more it appears that the unstressed adult body can conserve its vitamin B-6 very effectively and that the stores would last several months, perhaps much longer." Dr. Coburn noted that "growing children and physically stressed adults would lose pyridoxine more rapidly." This is accomplished by reducing the urinary loss of it.

THIAMIN

The body stores roughly 30 mg (*MNHD*, 8th edition, pg. 361) of thiamin. According to Vichai Tanphaichitr, MD, PhD, professor of medicine and director of the Research Center at the Ramathibodi Hospital, Bankok, Thailand, the "biological half-life of thiamin in the body is 9 to 18 days." In other words, it would take nine to eighteen days to utilize half of the stored 30 mg. Over the next nine to eighteen days, the body's efficiency at utilizing and conserving thiamin will rise, and only about half of the remaining 15 mg of stored thiamin would be used.

Only .5 mg of thiamin is needed for every 1,000 calories consumed. Thus, the average male may need 1 to 1.5 mg/day, and the average female 1.5 to 2 mg/day. Thiamin storage would last four weeks or longer.

B-12

The human body conserves vitamin B-12 very efficiently. Victor Herbert, MD, JD, an expert in folic acid and B-12 metabolism, wrote in *Modern Nutrition in Health and Disease*, "This almost total conservation of vitamin B-12 explains why pure vegetarians who eat almost no vitamin B-12 take decades to develop deficiency of the vitamin." The average B-12 stores in humans range from 2 to 5 mg, and "there is little evidence for significant catabolism, of vitamin

B-12, by man, and it is probable that loss occurs only by excretion, mainly in bile" (*MNHD*, 8th edition, pg. 408).

VITAMIN E

Ronald Sokol, MD, wrote about vitamin E in the text *Present Knowledge in Nutrition*, 7th edition. He explains that "symptomatic deficiency of vitamin E rarely, if ever, occurs in humans because of inadequate oral intake of the vitamin", probably due to its wide distribution in foods (pg. 132). Furthermore, Dr. Sokol notes that even "when malabsorption of vitamin E does occur in adults, it takes several years before plasma vitamin E levels decrease to a deficient range, because of the vitamin's presence in body stores" (pg. 132).

In their chapter on vitamin E in *Modern Nutrition in Health and Disease*, Phillip Furrell, MD, PhD, and Robert Roberts, MD, note that rapid development of vitamin E deficiency in humans apparently does not occur except in unusual clinical circumstances, and that the occurrence of vitamin E deficiency of pure dietary origin is rare in developed countries.

Recently, the Food and Nutrition Board recommended that the recommended daily intake for vitamin E be increased from 10 mg to 15 mg per day, even though millions of Americans maintain excellent health on one-third this amount. The late Max Horwitt, MD, a longtime vitamin E researcher, criticized the decision, stating that "more attention should have been paid to the amount of vitamin E consumed by millions of healthy individuals," which as he points out is about one-half of the 1989 RDA of 10 mg for adult males and 8 mg for adult females, "without any known apparent harm to the subjects evaluated." According to Dr. Horwitt, a supplement of vitamin E that provides more than "the amount greater than the RDA is a pharmacologic dose, not a nutritional requirement." A pharmacological dose is an intake of any nutrient above what is necessary for the prevention of disease and the maintenance of good health.

COPPER

The adult human body may contain only 20 to 50 mg copper (*MNHD*, 8th edition, pg. 234), but an adult's daily need is only 2 to 3 mg. Thus, even though the amount in storage may not appear to be significant, it is more than adequate to handle periods of reduced availability or increased need.

ZINC

The recommended level of zinc intake is 8 to 11 mg. But even with absorption of about 5 mg of zinc per day, the body can maintain storage of 1.5 to 2.5 grams, according to Robert Cousins, PhD, of the Center for Nutritional Sciences, University of Florida. While many people consume supplemental zinc to enhance their immune function, the May 2003 *Journal of Nutrition* stated that "high dosages of zinc evoke negative effects on immune cells and show alterations that are similar to those observed with zinc deficiency" (*Journal of Nutrition* 133: 1,452s–1,456s, May 2003).

Absorption Rates

Most of the digestion and absorption of food and its nutrients into the bloodstream occurs in the small intestine. The term small refers to its diameter, which is narrow (1 inch). The small intestine is lined with fingerlike projections called villi to enhance absorption. Each individual villus is made up of many absorptive cells, which increases the already 10 feet of absorptive length the nutrient must travel through "600 times beyond that of a simple tube" (*Contemporary Nutrition*, 6th edition, McGraw Hill, pg. 91). In short, the surface area to digest and absorb the required nutrients is enormous.

The transport of nutrients across the intestinal wall into the bloodstream can very dramatically depending upon need, availability, and negative interactions with other nutrients taken in excess, which may impede their absorption. As an example, large quantities of zinc can interfere with copper bioavailability (*MNHD*, 8th edition, pg. 216).

The authors of one research study showed that just 18.5 mg/day (slightly higher than the recommended 8 to 11 mg) of zinc for two weeks in young men reduced their copper availability (*Am J Clin Nutr* 1985; 41:285–292). This means that if you ingest a large supplemental dose of zinc with the belief that it may have some special health attributes, it may actually end up precipitating a health problem by reducing copper availability.

MAGNESIUM

When an individual's diet contains only 7 to 36 mg of magnesium (recommended levels are 310 to 400 mg/day depending upon age and gender), the body absorbs 67 to 70 percent of it and excretes little or no magnesium. However, when large amounts (100 mg or more) of magnesium are available in the diet, absorption rates drop to 11 to 14 percent (*MNHD*, 8th edition, pg. 168). With a self-selected diet, men on average absorb 21 percent and women 27 percent of magnesium from what is available from their food (*MNHD*, 8th edition, pg. 169). This means there is a significant buffer range for magnesium, and absorption rates can go up or down as needed.

IRON

Healthy individuals on a typical American diet absorb 5 to 10 percent of their intake of dietary iron (1 to 2 mg). When the body's iron stores are low (as during periods of increased need, such as pregnancy, or in iron-deficient patients), absorption rates increase to 10 to 20 percent (3 to 6 mg), which is two or three times greater than normal.

COPPER

A scientific paper from the Western Human Nutrition Research Center, San Francisco, and the Department of Nutrition, U.C. Davis, stated that "young men could maintain their copper status for forty-two days with a dietary copper intake of slightly less than 0.8 mg/day," well below the estimated safe intake of 1.5 to 3 mg/day according to the authors of the study (*Am J Clin Nutr* 1997; 65: 72–8) It seems that humans adapt to different amounts of copper in the diet by varying the body's efficiency of copper absorption.

According to this study, when dietary copper intake was 0.8 mg/day, absorption was 56 percent, which is much more efficient than with higher intakes. When intake was 7.5 mg/day, copper absorption was 12 percent, but when the intake was 1.7 mg/day, absorption soared to 36 percent.

In addition to changes in the efficiency of copper absorption, excretion of the body's copper stores was low when the dietary availability of copper was low, but excretion increased as the amount of dietary copper increased. According to the authors of this study, "[T]hese adaptations in absorption and endogenous [stored copper] excretion help prevent the development of copper deficiency when copper intake is low or toxicity when copper intake is high." However, if copper intake through supplementation is high for an extended period of time, such as 3 to 4 weeks, increased copper retention above normal will occur (*Am J Clin Nutr* 2005, 81: 822–828).

In her chapter on copper in the clinical text *Present Knowledge in Nutrition*, Maria Linder, PhD, of the Department of Chemistry and Biochemistry, California State University at Fullerton, wrote: "There appears to be an adaptation to levels of intake, so that there was a greater efficiency of absorption at lower intakes, and vice versa." Noting that an adult's actual need for copper may be less than 1 mg/day, Dr. Linder said there is little evidence of copper deficiency within the populations of industrialized nations.

Another expert, Judith Turnlund, PhD, with the USDA–ARS Western Human Nutrition Research Center, Davis, California, has stated that humans excrete little copper when dietary copper is low. She wrote in *Modern Nutrition in Health and Disease*, "The homeostatic regulation of copper absorption and excretion protects against copper deficiency and toxicity over a broad range of dietary intakes" (*MNHD*, 8th edition, pg. 234).

ZINC

The Department of Nutritional Sciences at the University of California, Berkeley, studied the zinc balancing capabilities of six young men who were confined while participating in a 75-day metabolic study. They were fed a diet providing either 16.5 mg zinc/day or 55 mg zinc/day. While receiving the 16.5 mg/day from the food, they absorbed about 25 percent of the zinc. When the diets availability of zinc was reduced to 5.5 mg/day, about one-half of what is recommended, absorption increased to about 53 percent after 13 days. (*J Nutr* 1985; 115:1,345–1,354).

Zinc supplements have become popular for the purported treatment of colds. However, on June 23, 2004, the nutrition newsletter *Nutrition News Focus* reiterated that "people taking a 45 mg supplement (for a total of 53 mg from supplements and diet) had decreased magnesium balance." The newsletter highlighted a well-controlled study that appeared in the May 2004 *European Journal of Clinical Nutrition*. The study demonstrated that moderately high zinc intake (roughly 50 mg), over six months, increased the excretion of magnesium in both urine and feces. "It also unfavorably altered two markers of bone formation" in the subjects of the study, sixty-five-year-old women.

Nutrition News Focus pointed out that "people taking zinc supplements or using zinc lozenges to treat cold symptoms can get up to 150 mg of zinc. These amounts can interfere with copper metabolism and depress HDL cholesterol and immune functions."

VITAMIN E

Vitamin E, one of the favored purported antioxidant supplements of many athletes and consumers in general, is commonly ingested in 200 to 400 mg dosages. "In normal humans, an average absorption of at least 50% and perhaps as high as 70% can be assumed for dietary levels of alpha-tocopherol consumption; however, the efficiency falls to less than 10% with pharmacological doses in the range of 200 mg" (*MNHD*, 8th edition, pg. 333).

CALCIUM

In studies described in *Modern Nutrition in Health and Disease*, when individuals went from consuming 2,000 mg/day of calcium to 300 mg/day, calcium absorption rates increased by 66 percent for women ages twenty-two to thirty-one and 50 percent for women ages sixty-one to seventy-five. The studies also appeared to indicate that 99.8 percent of calcium filtered by the kidneys is reabsorbed. (*MNHD*, 8th edition, pg. 152)

According to Lindsay Allen, PhD, RD, professor of nutritional sciences at the University of Connecticut, and Richard Wood, PhD, from the USDA Human Nutrition Research Center on Aging at Tufts University, who together wrote the *MNHD* chapter on calcium and phosphorous, "When calcium intake in human subjects is reduced abruptly from a high or adequate to a low level, within 1 week there is an increase in serum parathyroid hormone" (*MNHD*, 8th edition, pg. 152). This hormone increases the synthesis of the vitamin D hormone, which in turn increases the absorption of calcium by about 50% as one of its roles as well as a reduction in calcium excretion. This mechanism effectively compensates not only for low calcium intake but also for increased need, as in pregnant and lactating women.

In one study, researchers followed fourteen well-nourished women who consumed approximately 1,200 mg/day of calcium. The results showed that fetal calcium demand was met by increased intestinal absorption (*Am J Clin Nutr* 1998; 67(4):693–701).

Of course, there is a limit to the effectiveness of this absorption mechanism in the face of a poor diet over an extended period.

Research seems to indicate that most adult women need about 550 mg/day of calcium to prevent a negative calcium balance in storage; other studies suggest more than 550 mg/day is necessary. (But note that exercise is just as important as calcium intake—if not more so—for adolescents and young women to ensure maximum bone density after menopause.)

However, consider some comments attributed to Walter Willett, MD, DrPH, and chair of nutrition at the Harvard School of Public Health: "It is not clear how much calcium people need. Worldwide, consumption varies, and countries with average higher calcium intake tend to have higher rates of hip fractures. There is little proof that boosting calcium to currently recommended levels will prevent fractures, the principle complication of osteoporosis" (Interview with Lisa Ellis, published by *Intelihealth Health News*, August 8, 2001, "Rebuilding the Food Pyramid"). Dr. Willett has also stated that "most studies suggest that the older recommended level of 800 mg per day is adequate for most everyone. This is, in part, because the body has a good capacity to adjust the amount of calcium it can absorb from either diet or supplements depending on our needs." Current recommendations are 1,000 mg to 1,300 mg/day. Dr. Willett's comments are consistent with those of Dr. Max Horwitt concerning vitamin E and those of Dr. Alfred Harper concerning vitamin C; specifically, these experts agree that nutrient homeostasis appears to be maintained over a broad range of intakes, even those that fall considerably below the RDIs.

Excretion Rates

As noted earlier, many people believe that the body uses up nutrients and then quickly excretes or catabolizes what's left. This is a myth. Specifically, nutrient excretion rates readily change from rapid when intakes are excessive to very low when intake is low. Nutrient turnover is significantly reduced during times of increased need or decreased availability.

Another widely held myth is this: if a specific nutrient is associated with a specific reaction or beneficial biological role, then taking more of it will enhance that role. This simply is not true. To illustrate the fallacy of this idea, imagine for a moment that vitamins are keys. The keys are necessary to activate and/or regulate a wide variety of biological reactions, and they are needed in only very small amounts to perform these functions. When connected to the appropriate compounds, the keys may start a chain of reactions related to power and energy. However, the keys themselves do not provide the energy. The fuel (carbohydrates and fatty acids) do that. The vitamins assist in the process, but you cannot obtain more energy with more vitamins any more than your car could run faster or farther on a tank of gas if you had more ignition keys. The vitamins simply are one of the conduits that allow a series of reactions to begin or continue. The process cannot be accelerated or extended to provide more energy by taking additional vitamins. Excess vitamins are stored or excreted, just as an extra set of car keys would be set aside. Moreover, if the key is removed from the ignition, it can be reinserted and continue to start the vehicle many times before its usefulness is exhausted.

While this is an oversimplified analogy for an extensive and complex set of reactions in which all nutrients play a role, it's a good way to illustrate the body's recycling and reduced excretion mechanisms, which allow considerable latitude in daily nutrient intake.

The following examples demonstrate how dramatic changes in excretion rates can play a significant role in maintaining nutrient balance over a wide range of dietary intakes. However, keep in mind that this mechanism will not inherently protect those who foolishly ingest large doses of supplements. The copper information provided in Chapter 2 in the RDA section is a good example of how the excretion of excess nutrients may not be able to keep pace with excessive intakes from supplementation.

VITAMIN C

Robert Jacobs, PhD, wrote the chapter on vitamin C in the clinical nutrition text *Modern Nutrition in Health and Disease*, widely used in university nutrition courses. His research work has shown that when low intakes of nutrients occur, they are conserved in the tissues that need them the most. In a letter of 2/10/97, he stated, "Functional vitamin deficiency effects do not occur until tissue vitamin levels are nearly depleted, a process that generally takes 5 weeks or more."

In a study in which Dr. Jacobs's group gave eleven non-smoking male volunteers aged nineteen to thirty-two, just 5 mg/day of vitamin C (5.5 percent of the currently recommended 65 to 90 mg), blood plasma concentrations of vitamin C declined to less than one-fifth the original level. However, the concentration of vitamin C in the white blood cells (leukocytes) dropped by only 45 percent (*Am J Clin Nutr* 1987; 46:818–826).

"Leukocyte ascorbic acid levels reflect more accurately body or tissue stores of ascorbic acid than do plasma or erythrocyte levels," Dr. Jacobs noted. This is due to the white cell function's priority as a guard against oxidative damage to body tissue when the body's immune response causes the white cells to use oxygen to burn microbial invaders. These same cells are the first to be replenished when vitamin C intake increases. To simplify, the tissues which need vitamin C the most are the last to give it up during periods of low intake and the first to be restored when intakes increase.

Dr. Jacobs's results were supported by another study in which the daily vitamin C intake of seven healthy subjects was restricted to a mean daily intake of less than 3.9 mg/day. It took more than three weeks for the subjects' plasma concentrations of vitamin C to drop 70 percent (*Am J Clin Nutr* 1997; 65:1,434–1,440).

As noted in *Modern Nutrition in Health and Disease*, "In healthy prisoners depleted of ascorbic acid, the catabolic rate [or breakdown rate] decreased from 45 mg/day at an initial body pool of

1500 mg, to 9 mg/day at a pool size of 300 mg. Overall, the body turnover of ascorbic acid amounted to about 3% of the existing body pool per day."

The text *Present Knowledge in Nutrition* has this to say: "When doses of ascorbate is less than 100 mg, no ascorbate is excreted in the urine. By contrast, at steady-state [chronic intakes for doses greater than or equal to 500 mg] all of the absorbed dose is excreted in urine" (*PKN*, 7th edition, pg. 155). At 100 mg, about a quarter of the dose is excreted, and at 200 mg, the figure rises to half (pg. 152). At higher doses of vitamin C, virtually all the absorbed dose is excreted.

PYRIDOXINE (B-6)

According to pyridoxine expert Stephen Coburn, PhD, in a 2/17/97 letter, it appears that if an intake of .5 mg/day of vitamin B-6 (one-third of the RDA) or more is available, adults who are not under any physiological stress (such as illness, pregnancy, or lactation) can reduce their urinary losses and balance their intake of vitamin B-6.

RIBOFLAVIN

Several published studies have demonstrated that when riboflavin needs are increased as a result of increased physical work, a simultaneous reduction in riboflavin excretion in the urine occurs to accommodate the increased need (*J Nutr* 1960; 72:251–261, and *Am J Clin Nutr* 1983; 37:509–517).

FOLATE

The excretion rates of folate decline in pregnant women and those who are breastfeeding as their need increases. There is a decline in urinary excretion of folate during the second trimester of pregnancy, which implies that pregnant women may be more efficient at conserving folate than nonpregnant women due to increased needs of the fetus (*J Nutr* 1998; 128 (2):204–208).

SELENIUM

According to *Present Knowledge in Nutrition*, metabolic balance can be achieved with a wide range of selenium intakes (anywhere from 9 to 80 ug/day). The data, derived from studies in China, New Zealand, and the United States, showed that individuals with reduced selenium intake maintained their nutrient balance by decreasing urinary and fecal excretion of selenium (*PKN*, 7th edition, pg. 325).

MOLYBDENUM

Dr. Judith Turnlund studied the ability of healthy young men to maintain molybdenum balance over a very wide intake, ranging from just 22 mg/day to 1,490 mg/day for twenty-four days each. Dr. Turnland and her colleagues at the USDA, ARS/Western Nutrition Research Center, concluded that "molybdenum retention is regulated by urinary excretion. Molybdenum is conserved at low intakes and excess molybdenum is rapidly excreted in the urine when intake is high" (*Am J Clin Nutr* 1995; 62 (4):790–6).

MAGNESIUM

When magnesium intake is severely restricted in individuals with normal kidney function, the output of magnesium becomes small within five to seven days, according to Maurice Shils, MD, ScD, adjunct professor of public health sciences at Bowman Gray School of Medicine, Wake Forest University. Writing in *Modern Nutrition in Health and Disease*, Dr. Shils noted that in normal individuals, intestinal and renal conservation and excretory mechanisms keep a balance over a wide dietary intake.

Consider a study reported in the *Journal of Nutrition* that illustrated that both "urinary and fecal magnesium losses decreased significantly (30 and 40 percent respectively) with dietary magnesium restriction (93 days) (*J Nutr* 132: 930–935, 2002). Specifically, magnesium intake was reduced to 155 mg/day, which resulted in impaired work economy for these forty-five- to seventy-one-year-old women. During the very low magnesium diet, the subjects required increased oxygen utilization to accomplish the same work output. Keep in mind that these subjects were ingesting one half of what is recommended for three months.

ZINC

In a study reported in the *American Journal of Clinical Nutrition* in which zinc intake was severely reduced (.3 mg/day), fecal loss of zinc was reduced from more than 10 mg/day to less than 1 mg/day (*Am J Clin Nutr* 1984; 39:556–579).

The same journal reported similar results in 2004. In a study of healthy nine- to fourteen-year-old girls, a low zinc diet was introduced for two weeks; the girls' fecal excretion of zinc was again significantly reduced (*Am J Clin Nutr* 2004; 80:385–390).

MANGANESE

John Finley, PhD, with the USDA Agricultural Research Service, studied the absorption and retention rates of manganese among twenty-six healthy, nonpregnant women, ages twenty to forty-five (*Am J Clin Nutr* 1999; 70:37–43). The women consumed either a low- or high-manganese diet for thirty days. Those on the low-manganese diet received a mean of only .75 mg/day; those on the high-manganese diet ranged from 8.9 to 9.2 mg/day. A small tracer dose of radioactive manganese was given to permit tracing of manganese. The study showed the following results:

1. Despite large differences in intake, the body effectively controlled the ultimate retention of manganese.
2. The calculated percentage retention of radioactive manganese after sixty days was five to ten times greater in those eating the low-manganese diet than those with the high-manganese diet.

3. Excretion is an important means of controlling the balance of manganese; excretion rates declined dramatically to compensate for reduced intake.
4. Subjects in this study were consuming manganese intakes that were below or in excess of the estimated safe and adequate daily dietary intake; however, their clinical measures of manganese were not substantially changed. (This does not mean that in extreme cases over a prolonged period, problems could not develop in individuals deprived of adequate manganese.)

In closing, consumers will repeatedly hear that study after study has demonstrated that the average American's diet is insufficient in one nutrient or another based upon current recommendations. It is true that most Americans certainly need to improve their dietary habits but it must be kept in mind that this data must be interpreted with caution. Any deficiency estimates based solely upon intake data can be misleading due to each individual's ability to adapt to a certain extent to low intakes for short periods of time and still maintain a healthy balance.

4 ANTIOXIDANTS

"MAGIC BULLET," OR MORE DECEPTION?

According to the American Heart Association, as many as 30 percent of Americans are taking some form of antioxidant supplement. Antioxidants have been called a "magic bullet" and given credit for everything from slowing the aging process to boosting the immune system, assisting in the recovery of muscle tissue between workouts, and preventing some diseases. However, before stocking up on a supply of antioxidant dietary supplements, consider these facts:

- The National Cancer Institute does not recommend antioxidants to prevent cancer.
- The American Cancer Society does not recommend antioxidants to prevent cancer and states that individuals with lung cancer, particularly, should not take beta-carotene.
- The American Heart Association does not recommend antioxidants to prevent heart disease.
- The U.S. Preventive Services Task Force (USPSTF), an independent panel of health care experts, does not recommend antioxidants to prevent either cancer or heart disease; the USPSTF

also states that beta-carotene either alone or in combination with other supplemental antioxidants "might cause harm in some groups, specifically smokers" (http://www.ahrq.gov/clinic/uspstf/uspsvita.htm).

- The American College of Sports Medicine (ACSM) does not recommend antioxidants to improve athletic performance or to assist in muscle recovery.
- The American Council on Science and Health does not recommend antioxidants.

So what do these major science organizations know that the general public does not?

Exactly What Are Antioxidants?

The human body naturally produces certain chemicals, called free radicals, that oxidize cells. While this oxidation is a normal body function, in excess it causes permanent damage and leaves the body more vulnerable to the effects of aging and to certain diseases. Luckily, the body also has a natural antioxidant function that combats this cell damage. Other antioxidants, including vitamins E and C, beta-carotene, glutathione, and superoxide dismutase, are found in foods. This class of compounds includes hundreds, if not thousands, of plant compounds (phytochemicals)—most of which have not been fully identified or studied, that play a vital role in our health. And many of these compounds' biological roles are unrelated to their standard classification as an antioxidant or stabilizers of free radicals.

Consider the following comment published by the American Institute for Cancer Research in an August 31, 2000, press release: "Although hundreds of vitamins, minerals and herbal compounds are now available in supplement form, food scientists estimate that fruits, vegetables, whole grains and beans could contain thousands of yet-to-be identified substances. Further, the naturally occurring compounds within these foods interact in complex ways that science is only beginning to understand." In other words, the classic compounds marketed as antioxidants have a plethora of currently unknown functions. Under certain circumstances, such as when they are consumed in excess, they might actually *promote* the production of free radicals and displace other biologically active compounds from storage.

The supplement industry has jumped enthusiastically onto the antioxidant bandwagon, oversimplifying these compounds and their functions to promote sales. North Americans now spend more than $1 billion per year on vitamin E supplementation alone (*Contemporary Nutrition*, 6th edition, pg. 24). The vast majority of this is consumed as the alpha-tocopherol form of vitamin E. Most consumers do not understand that alpha-tocopherol is only one of at least *eight* forms of vitamin E available in food. In fact, there are four tocopherol forms (alpha, beta, gamma, delta) of vitamin E, plus four tocotrienol forms.

The tocotrienols, as well as all naturally occurring vitamin E forms, have their own unique biological activities. This is a very significant point, because the overutilization, through supplementation, of one form of the vitamin may actually *displace* the absorption, storage, and utilization of other forms.

Similarly, when you reach for your beta-carotene supplement, remember that the beta form is only one of hundreds, possibly thousands, of naturally occurring carotenoids available from food.

The marketing of antioxidant supplements as a method for improving your health as well as your athletic performance, recovery, and physical development is an oversimplification of a very complex system of checks and balances—a system that is best served by eating a wide variety of fruits, vegetables, and grains. Foods contain hundreds of compounds which work synergistically with each other to produce the desired healthful benefits.

As pointed out by the American Council on Science and Health, "[A]ntioxidants in foods may have to work in concert with other ingredients in order to have a beneficial effect." The supplementation in high dosages of the popular antioxidants vitamin E, C, and beta-carotene might disrupt the normal balance of these compounds as well as the balance of free radicals in the body and cause more harm than good.

There are hundreds, if not thousands, of naturally occurring antioxidants in food. We have very little understanding of most of these, and thus it is impossible for any supplement manufacturer to have a clue as to what really constitutes a "complete antioxidant formula"—although many attempt to market them. As an example, after researchers gathered for an international conference on a group of plant compounds called polyphenols, a scientific report on the researchers' opinions stated that "polyphenols in foods are more complex than often thought" (*Am J Clin Nutr* 2005; 81: 223S–229S).

Our understanding of antioxidant compounds, how many there are, and what they do is minimal. For example, betalains are recently identified naturally occurring compounds that do have antioxidant activity. However, little is known regarding betalains' exact availability, their biological roles, or whether large supplemental intakes of other compounds will inhibit betalains' absorption and bioavailability.

Antioxidants' purported benefits are theoretically related to the inhibition of the potentially destructive effects of excess free radical production on human tissues. Take note, however, of the qualifiers here: *purported, theoretically, potentially.* There is good reason to be cautious about antioxidant supplements. As is the case across the board in the supplement industry, many of the advertising claims related to antioxidants are riddled with fallacies and overstatements. Most importantly, unwary individuals who believe these statements or who follow the bad advice of their peers and megadose with antioxidants risk real physical harm.

No matter how persuasive the pitch from the supplement industry, no fabricated product can replace *real food.* This is particularly true for antioxidants, which scientists do not yet fully understand. For example, we do not know the full antioxidant potential of the average fruit or vegetable. A 1998 *Consumer Reports* publication noted that the antioxidants vitamin C, vitamin E, and beta-carotene account for only 15 percent of the total antioxidant potency contained in a fruit or vegetable; the other 85 percent of the antioxidant potential comes from relatively obscure plant chemicals.

The June 2004 *American Journal of Clinical Nutrition* reported on a twenty-five-day study that demonstrated that the biomarkers (a substance found in the blood that can be used to evaluate the effectiveness of a treatment or supplement) of oxidative damage to protein and lipids (fats) were significantly lower in individuals consuming 600 grams of fruits and vegetables per day compared to individuals who took a pill containing the vitamins and minerals corresponding to those in 600 grams of fruit and vegetables.

Expert Input

Cornell University news release of June 21, 2000, on the research of Dr. Rui Hai Liu, an assistant professor of food science.

"The researchers found that the vitamin C in apples is responsible for only a small portion of the antioxidant activity. Instead, almost all of this activity in apples is from phytochemicals. Indeed previous studies have shown that a 500 milligram vitamin C pill might act as a pro-oxidant. This study demonstrated that the combination of phytochemicals plays a very important role in antioxidant and anti-cancer activity, with the real health benefits coming from a phytochemical mixture."

Dr. Liu stated "Scientists are interested in isolating single compounds—such as vitamin C, vitamin E and beta carotene—to see if they exhibit anti-oxidant or anti-cancer benefits. It turns out that none of those works alone to reduce cancer. It's the combination of flavonoids and polyphenols doing the work."

> Cornell researchers "found that eating 100 grams of fresh apple with skins provided a total antioxidant activity equal to 1,500 mg of vitamin C." Eating fruits and vegetables is better than taking a vitamin pill. "Previous studies have shown that a 500-mg vitamin C pill might act as a pro-oxidant." A pro-oxidant is a molecule that promotes oxidation of other molecules by accepting its electrons, such as free radicals. However, you can obtain enough antioxidants from food without worrying about toxicity, Dr. Liu stated.

In March 1, 2005 Cornell University News Service released another report regarding Dr. Liu's ongoing research with the disease-fighting phytochemicals in apples. In this report Dr. Liu states "that the thousands of phytochemicals in foods vary in molecular size, polarity and solubility, which could affect how they are absorbed and distributed in different cells, tissues and organs. This balanced natural combination of phytochemicals present in fruits and vegetables cannot simply be mimicked by dietary supplements."

The same report quotes David R. Jacobs, professor in the Division of Epidemiology, School of Public Health, University of Minnesota: "Dr. Liu is in the forefront of a group of investigators, including myself, who find extensive evidence that extremely important health aspects of food work through the combination of substances that make up that food, a concept we call food synergy. Risk of many chronic diseases in modern life appears to be reduced by whole foods, but not by isolated large doses of selected food compounds."

Understanding Free Radicals

Supplementing the diet with antioxidants to "control" free-radical production is a simple-minded approach to a very complex process. Free radicals have unfairly become synonymous with tissue damage, decay, aging, cancer, and death. In fact, they are a normal by-product of many biological processes, and the body requires a balance between normal and excessive production of free radicals in order to maintain good health. Free radicals are part of our cells' everyday life.

Free radicals are molecules that are missing an electron and looking to acquire another to replace it. To do this, free radicals react with other molecules to acquire one of their electrons; this, in turn, destabilizes and possibly damages the molecule that transferred its electron to the free radical. Nutrients with an antioxidant function as one of their many biological roles, such as vitamin E and C, neutralize these compounds by giving up one of their electrons to the free radical, stabilizing it and preventing it from disrupting the integrity of structural cells.

Through physical training, athletes naturally enhance their bodies' own antioxidant capabilities. But when free radicals are unrestrained, which can occur in cases of disease but not in healthy individuals, they can progressively destroy and alter the function of cells, or they can excessively oxidize fatty acids in the blood or cell membranes. This damage to the body can lead to cancer, heart disease, aging, and muscle damage in some individuals.

Advertisers of antioxidants do a wonderful job of instilling fear in consumers by directly associating free radicals with the development of chronic diseases or muscle tissue damage. This leads millions of consumers to rationalize, "Why not load up on antioxidants and get rid of as many free radicals as possible?" Remember: free radicals are not always harmful, and they do have a significant positive biological role.

Expert Input

From the chapter on antioxidants in the clinical textbook *Present Knowledge in Nutrition*, pg. 597.

Many free radicals perform essential biological functions. For example, "The phagocyte cells (neutrophils, monocytes, macrophages,

> and eosinophils) that defend the body against bacteria, viruses and fungi generate large amounts of superoxide (a free radical) as part of the mechanism by which foreign organisms are killed. This is an essential defense mechanism against infection."
>
> Additionally, the free radical nitric oxide "performs many useful physiological functions, such as regulation of blood pressure and intercellular signaling."

Free radicals are critical in the production of certain hormones; in addition, they likely have many positive roles we are unaware of. In support of this, consider the "Position Statement on Human Aging" published by *Scientific American* on May 13, 2002, which stated that "the purpose of this document is to warn the public against the use of ineffective and potentially harmful antiaging interventions and to provide a brief but authoritative consensus statement from 51 internationally recognized scientists in the field about what we know and do not know about intervening in human aging."

In the section on antioxidants, this report included the following statement:

> *The scientifically respected free-radical theory of aging serves as a basis for the prominent role that antioxidants have in the antiaging movement. The claim that ingesting supplements containing antioxidants can influence aging is often used to sell antiaging formulations. The logic used by their proponents reflects a misunderstanding of how cells detect and repair the damage caused by free radicals and the important role that free radicals play in normal physiological processes (such as immune response and cell communication). Nevertheless, there is little doubt that ingesting fruits and vegetables (which contain antioxidants) can reduce the risk of having various age-associated diseases, such as cancer, heart disease, macular degeneration and cataracts. At*

present there is relatively little evidence from human studies that supplements containing antioxidants lead to a reduction in either the risk of these conditions or the rate of aging . . . the possible adverse effects of single-dose supplements, such as beta-carotene, caution against their indiscriminate use. As such, antioxidant supplements may have some health benefits for some people, but so far there is no scientific evidence to justify the claim that they have any effect on human aging."

A research group at the University College, London, cast further doubt on the theory that free radicals are directly responsible for disease and that supplemental antioxidants help prevent it. In their study, published in February 2004 in *Nature,* the researchers pointed out that the production of free radicals by white blood cells is essential for the efficient killing of microbes, such as fungi. However, they demonstrated that it was enzymes, not free radicals, that gave the white blood cells their destructive power. When a chemical blocked certain enzymes, the white blood cells lost their ability to kill microbes.

Simply put, it may *not* be an oxidative process that destroys tissue, but an enzymatic or unrelated process yet to be determined. Nevertheless, millions of consumers routinely ingest antioxidant supplements without having any idea of what they might be tampering with. And you can bet you won't see antioxidants' potential negative effects mentioned in advertising.

No Magic Bullets

The supplement industry bombards the public with advertising suggesting that vitamins E, C, and beta-carotene are the "magic bullets" of antioxidants. Taking them in supplement form is supposed to protect the consumer against a variety of conditions, the "natural" way. But there is nothing "natural" about supplements. As Ritva Butrum, PhD, vice president for research at the American

Institute for Cancer Research, has stated, "There is no such thing as a natural supplement. It is a contradiction of terms. The natural thing would be to get these substances in the combinations and amounts that occur in a healthy, balanced diet. There is nothing remotely natural about a supplement containing a single compound in amounts five, ten, or twenty times greater than anything found in nature" (AICR press release, March 6, 2000, "Magic Bullet Supplements Unlikely to Prevent Cancer").

The Cornell University research involving apples mentioned earlier studied colon cancer cells that were treated with apple extracts. The biggest effect (inhibition of the growth of these cells) was seen in the cells that were treated with extracts from both the skin and the fleshy part of the apple. There can be no doubt that those eating apples and other fruits and vegetables get a greater benefit than those using dietary supplements.

And remember that vitamin C is only one of the plant chemicals found in an apple. On your next trip to the grocery store, weigh one small Red Delicious apple. Most weigh roughly one-quarter pound, a little over 100 grams (one pound = 454 grams). An apple this size contains approximately 8 mg of vitamin C. The remaining chemicals in that apple play as important a role—if not more important—in the apple's total antioxidant function.

A similar study was published in the American Institute for Cancer Research newsletter (Fall 2000, pg. 8). The report, "Phytochemical Watch—Resveratrol Helps Prevent Cancer, Heart Disease," stated that the plant compound resveratrol "seems to fight cancer many different ways." Its functions may include "blocking the action of cancer-causing agents, inhibiting the development and growth of tumors, and causing pre-cancerous cells to revert to normal." However, the report noted that research on this compound has been limited to cell cultures and animal studies and stated that it is "unknown if results will be similar in humans." Again, until more is known about this compound, it would be unwise to consume large amounts in supplement form. According to the newsletter report, "[R]esearchers caution against consuming large amounts of resveratrol in supplement form. Resveratrol has a similar molecular structure to estrogen and could have undesirable side effects, including stimulating the growth of breast cancer cells. Reaching a dangerously high level of consumption, however, would be nearly impossible through consuming resveratrol in foods and beverages." Resveratrol is reportedly found in at least seventy-two different plants, with grapes and grape products among the richest sources.

Clearly, there are no magic bullets to replace wise food choices.

Expert Input

Victor Herbert, MD, late professor of medicine at Mt. Sinai School of Medicine, New York City, writing in the *American Journal of Clinical Nutrition* (1994).

Consider the following comments by Dr. Victor Herbert, recognized as an expert by the Federation of American Societies for Experimental Biology: "The nutrient buzzword for 1994 is 'antioxidant.' Every supplement so labeled is seen as having only an upside and no downside. This is a myth. No supplement is a pure antioxidant.

"At the November 1993 Food and Drug Administration Conference on Antioxidant Vitamins in Cancer and Cardiovascular Disease, there was essentially unanimous agreement that vitamins C, E, and B-carotene are mischaracterized when they are described solely as 'antioxidants' (fighters against harmful free radicals). What they are, in fact, is redox agents, antioxidant in some circumstances (often so in the physiological quantities found in food), and pro-oxidant (producing billions of harmful free radicals) in other circumstances (often so in the pharmacological quantities found in supplements).

> "Large doses of vitamin E enhance immune activity and thus may promote progression of immune and autoimmune disease (i.e. asthma, food allergy, diabetes, rheumatoid arthritis, multiple sclerosis, and lupus)."
>
> "Vitamin C is especially dangerous in the presence of high body iron stores, which make vitamin C violently pro-oxidant. For genetic reasons, more than 10% of American Caucasians and perhaps as many as 30% of American blacks have high body iron," a condition called hemochromatosis. For consumer protection, every advertisement and label for vitamin C and/or iron supplements should warn: Do not take this product until your blood iron status has been determined.
>
> "We recently reported that in the presence of iron, not only does vitamin C appear to be worthless again cancer, but it increased lipoxidation of relatively harmless low-density-lipoprotein (LDL) cholesterol to coronary-artery-damaging oxidized LDL cholesterol."
>
> Because vitamin C has the ability to release or mobilize stored iron in the body, taking heavy vitamin C supplementation could cause iron release into the blood beyond the iron binding capacity. The resulting free iron could have severe consequences to heart tissue from iron overload.
>
> Dr. Herbert also pointed out that the vitamin C in a supplement would not have the same effect as the vitamin C found in food, as an example, a glass of orange juice. He points out that food always contains a balance of the natural mixture of vitamin C biochemistry, both oxidized and reduced forms, whereas supplements do not, which he describes as "unbalanced biochemistry."

In January 2004, the *Nutrition Journal* published a review entitled "Iron supplements: the quick fix with long-term consequences," from the School of Pharmacy and Biomolecular Sciences, University of Brighton, UK. In this review, the authors make several important points:

1. Vitamin C has been shown to exhibit antioxidant effects at low doses but conversely at high doses it becomes a pro-oxidant.
2. The high intake of iron or vitamin C alone warrants serious consideration. In tandem this cocktail is potent. Uncontrolled interaction between vitamin C and iron salts [free or unbound iron] leads to oxidative stress.
3. Supplementing iron with vitamin C exacerbates oxidative stress in the gastrointestinal tract leading to ulceration in healthy individuals.
4. Further studies need to be conducted to examine the detrimental effects of neutraceuticals especially in chronic inflammatory conditions.
5. High tissue concentrations of iron are associated with a number of pathologies including some cancers, inflammation, diabetes, liver and heart disease (http://www.nutritionj.com/content/3/1/2).

The points Dr. Herbert and the *Nutrition Journal* article make are considerations for athletes and consumers, especially males. Iron losses from the body are small and most of it is recycled from molecules which contain it. Females will lose iron each month through menstruation and it is not uncommon for low meat eating or vegetarian women to be anemic. However, for males, the main and only real regulation of iron is through its absorption from the intestines. If iron absorption exceeds the very small excretion rates of it through greater absorption, the long-term health consequences can be very serious.

The typical American diet is already too high in protein, and most athletes consume even higher quantities due to the misunderstanding of just how little protein is actually in one pound of muscle tissue (only 22 percent or 100 grams; see the protein chapter for details). The resulting excess protein intake as well as iron in tandem with large doses of supplemental vitamin C as part of their "antioxidant" muscle recovery cocktail may lead to excessive iron absorption and retention even without the genetic disorder hemochromatosis.

According to the Centers for Disease Control and Prevention (CDC), the hereditary disorder hemochromatosis is one of the most common genetic disorders. The CDC states that some of the disorders associated with this disease are arthritis, cirrhosis of the liver, diabetes, heart failure, and liver cancer ("CDC Nutrition & Physical Activity Overview on Iron Overload and Hemochromatosis"). Individuals who have been diagnosed with this condition should be extremely cautious about taking vitamin C supplements. The booklet *Facts About Hemochromatosis*, prepared by the Hemochromatosis Foundation states that a normal adult stores about 4 grams of iron, while someone with hemochromatosis can store 20 to 40 grams or more. It also states that an estimated 1.5 million Americans are affected by the disease, with a carrier population of between 25 and 30 million. The foundation warns that these individuals should "avoid alcohol, vitamin supplements, especially vitamin C, which can increase iron toxicity."

A May 1998 American College of Sports Medicine report on vitamin and mineral supplements and exercise stated that "chronic ingestion of large doses of ascorbic acid can produce physiological disturbances. Some examples include renal stone formation, decreased coagulation time, erythrocyte hemolysis, and gastrointestinal disturbances. It was recently suggested that the iron-overload induced cardiac deaths of three athletes may have been precipitated by megadose supplements of vitamin C."

Displacement of Stored Antioxidants

Researchers have known for many years that excessive intakes of the alpha form of vitamin E can displace other forms of the vitamin. In 1994 researchers at the Department of Molecular and Cell Biology at the University of California at Berkeley reported the displacement of stored gamma-tocopherol with the alpha form (found in supplements) with as little as 250 mg per day (*Am J Clin Nutr* 1994; 59: 1,025–1,032).

In 1997 researchers examined the effects of alpha-tocopherol supplements on the storage of the gamma form in skeletal muscle tissue. The subjects were given 800 IU of alpha-tocopherol per day for thirty days. The researchers found that the alpha supplements displaced the gamma storage not only in the skeletal muscle but also in the plasma, where the alpha form increased 300 percent while the gamma form decreased 74 percent over a fifteen-day period (Meydani M., et al, *J Nutr Biochem* 1997; 8: 74–78).

A number of free radicals are not neutralized by alpha-tocopherol. They respond instead to gamma-tocopherol, which is found in food (specifically in nuts, grain, and soybeans), but not in most supplements. This data was reported in the April 1997 Proceedings of the National Academy of Sciences by Stephen Christen, PhD, a biochemist and researcher at the University of California at Berkeley. He noted that only gamma-tocopherol neutralizes peroxynitrite, a very destructive free radical found at inflammation sites, a common occurrence in athletes who routinely overwork muscle tissue and their tendons. In addition, gamma-tocopherol appears to be responsible for the neutralization of nitrogen oxide, a common air pollutant. Athletes who train in polluted regions of the country should keep this in mind when they supplement with large doses of alpha-tocopherol.

The Federation of American Societies for Experimental Biology Online Journal also reported on this potentially significant problem of supplemental vitamin E displacing other biologically important forms. This 2002 study demonstrated that the gamma form of vitamin E demonstrated a more significant growth inhibition or anticancer activity on prostate, colorectal, and bone cancer cells than did the alpha form found in most supplements, which the authors speculated was unrelated to *any* antioxidant activity. Remember, all nutrients are involved in more than one specific task (*FASEB Journal Express*, Article doi:10, 1096/fj.02-0362fje October 4, 2002). Tocotrienol, another form of vitamin E, has also been reported to inhibit certain types of cancer cells that are unaffected by alpha-tocopherol.

It also appears that vitamin C supplements can displace other naturally produced antioxidants. In a study published in the journal *Free Radical Biology and Medicine*, the authors demonstrated that oral vitamin C supplements of 500 mg/day for eight weeks resulted in the reduction of several other antioxidants normally found and stored in skin cells (*Free Radical Biology & Medicine*, 2002; 33 (10): pp. 1,355–1,362). The January 22, 2003, issue of the newsletter *Nutrition News Focus* commented on this finding: "The antioxidants produced by the body are probably more important in protecting against radical damage than vitamin C. This seems another reason to avoid that aisle in the pharmacy."

Some research has shown that, in addition to alpha-tocopherol's ability to displace other forms of vitamin E, it is also capable of displacing other antioxidants. In June 2000, the *Journal of the American College of Nutrition* reported that "supplementation with vitamin E (400 IU/day) caused significant drops in carotenoids in the LDL, which are also thought to prevent against oxidation. Both beta-carotene and lycopene decrease significantly at eight weeks."

Low-density lipoproteins (LDL) are molecules in the blood which contain a large proportion of cholesterol and transport lipids (fat) from the liver to other tissues in the body such as fat and muscle. LDLs are often referred to as the "bad cholesterol" due to their association to an increased risk for heart disease or stroke when elevated. The point is if supplemental vitamin E is displacing carotenoids and the resulting decreased balance of various antioxidants in the LDLs, then the oxidation of the LDL molecule may increase as well, exacerbating its potential for precipitating heart disease or strokes.

A review article in the *American Journal of Clinical Nutrition* entitled "Gamma-tocopherol, the Major Form of Vitamin E in the U.S. Diet, Deserves More Attention," made the following points:

- Gamma-tocopherol constitutes as much as 30 to 50 percent of the total vitamin E contained in human skin, muscle, vein, and adipose tissue.
- It is well documented that plasma and tissue gamma-tocopherol are suppressed by alpha-tocopherol supplementation.
- Gamma-tocopherol has more affinity, due to its chemical structure, to trap certain reactive molecules, such as various nitrogen oxide species. Excess generation of these molecules is associated with chronic inflammation-related diseases, such as cancer, cardiovascular disease, and neurodegenerative disorders.
- Gamma-tocopherol is superior to alpha-tocopherol in detoxifying nitrogen dioxide.
- Some studies suggest that gamma-tocopherol may play a role in preventing type 1 diabetes.
- The regular consumption of nuts, which are an excellent source of gamma-tocopherol, lowers the risk of myocardial infarction and death from ischemic heart disease. (*Am J Clin Nutr* 2001; 74: 714–722).

Why Do Consumers and Athletes Believe They Need Supplemental Antioxidants?

Misinformation, misunderstandings, and some blatantly deceptive marketing practices have convinced many active consumers that antioxidant supplements will provide the following benefits:

- enhanced muscle recovery after exercise,
- prevention of exercise-induced muscle damage, and
- enhanced immunity.

ENHANCED MUSCLE RECOVERY

Many athletes firmly believe that taking antioxidant supplements will help them both to recover more quickly from their physical workouts and to sustain less muscle damage by reducing or diminishing the impact of free radicals. However, a report in the *Journal of Medicine and Science in Sports and Exercise* said that free radical production during the course of intense exercise is as likely to be a mediating or necessary factor for the remodeling of tissue after exercise as it is to be an unwanted by-product. Eliminating too many free radicals could actually *harm* performance and health.

The ACSM is not alone regarding the necessity of free radicals to assist in the stimulation of stressed muscle tissue to adapt. The *Journal of Anatomy* stated that the increase in exercise-induced free-radicals in "the muscle may act as a signal for adaptation" (J. Anat 2000 Nov; 197 Pt 4: 539–41). In 1999, *The Proceedings of the Nutrition Society* published an article entitled "Free radicals in skin and muscle: damaging agents or signals for adaptation?" The article stated "There is increasing evidence that free radicals act as signals for cell adaptation in a variety of cell types . . ."(Vol. 58, 3, 1999, 673–676 (4).)

Consistent with this view is a statement made by researchers from the University of Bath in a study that appeared in the *European Journal of Applied Physiology* in 2003. The study, which examined postexercise vitamin C supplementation and recovery from demanding exercise, suggested that perhaps "free radicals are not involved in delaying the recovery process following a bout of unaccustomed exercise" (*Eur J Appl Physiol* 2003, 89: 393–400). In fact, the most beneficial thing athletes can do to enhance muscle recovery after exercise, besides appropriate rest, is to consume sufficient carbohydrates from fruits, vegetables, and whole grains, which bring with them all the naturally occurring compounds.

On September 27, 2001, the *Daily University Science News* published a report entitled "Body May Rust Inside If Vitamin C Over Maximum Dose." The report, reprinted verbatim here, directly disputes the theory of enhancing muscle recovery after exercise with supplemental antioxidants:

"If you have a bruise, a muscle sprain, an inflammatory disease or if you take iron supplements, exceeding 100 mg per day of vitamin C may be damaging to your body, according to a study by University of Florida researchers.

"That is because all those conditions produce free iron, which reacts negatively with vitamin C in muscle the same way that the iron on bicycles and fences reacts with water and oxygen.

"'You will rust inside, so to speak,' says Christiaan Leeuwenburgh, the senior author and an assistant professor of the University of Florida's department of exercise and sport sciences.

"In a study published this month in the journal *Free Radical Biology and Medicine,* several UF researchers worked with renowned vitamin C expert Barry Halliwell to test the effects of vitamin C and N-acetyl-cysteine (NAC, another water-soluble antioxidant) at the cellular level.

"In this study, the researchers began with the hypothesis that vitamin C and NAC would speed the recovery of a muscle injury because of their antioxidant properties and ability to reach damaged cells quickly.

"Fourteen healthy men volunteered to have one of their arms injured by a machine, which injured their bicep muscles and creating swelling. Researchers then gave half of them a placebo and the other half a drink supplemented with about 700 mg of vitamin C and 800 mg of NAC.

"'Initially, the vitamin C and NAC were given to prevent the injury, because we thought they would have protective effects,' Leeuwenburgh said. 'Instead, they were damaging.'

"Leeuwenburgh attributes the damaging effects of the vitamin C and NAC to their reaction with iron in the body. Normally, iron is bound to proteins and enzymes and therefore cannot react with vitamin C and NAC.

"But when inflammation occurs—as it does in muscular injuries and a variety of diseases such as Alzheimer's, arthritis and cardiovascular disease—the body releases more free iron, which is highly reactive to outside elements—in this case, vitamin C and NAC. Indeed, the researchers showed that there were increases in free iron following this type of exercise.

"'Vitamin C isn't bad, and neither is NAC, but by some mechanism in this situation there were some pro-oxidant effects of supplementation,' said April Childs, a graduate student in the department of exercise and sport sciences and the lead author of the study.

"In addition, although Leeuwenburgh says people who have taken vitamin C or NAC in the past should not worry too much about the new finding, he recommends caution in supplementing vitamin C in doses greater than 100 mg after injuries or disease condition characterized by increases in free iron.

"'People should limit their vitamin C intake until we know more,' he said. 'Everyone agrees that after 80 to 90 milligrams, about the recommended daily allowance, it goes out of your body since measurements show that white blood cells are saturated completely after this dose. You would think that if it goes out of your body it is not harmful, but maybe the high transient levels do react in a negative way. There's no benefit to taking more than the RDA, and it could actually harm you.'

"Furthermore, he said, 'Vitamin C is believed to prevent cancer, but instead, it may be damaging. Studies performed on humans actually show that it may increase DNA damage.'

"Because vitamin C and NAC in the body appear to react most negatively with iron, Leeuwenburgh said, those with inflammatory diseases and those who take more than the recommended daily allowance of iron should be particularly vigilant about limiting their vitamin C and NAC intake.

"'If you're taking more than the RDA of iron, you're putting yourself at risk by taking more than the RDA of vitamin C or NAC at the same time,' Leeuwenburgh said. 'Iron is very important in preventing anemia. So many people—particularly women—are supplementing, and the effects of supplementing iron and vitamin C for long periods have not been adequately studied.'

"'Therefore, to supplement vitamin C and iron together may be damaging. Further studies are required to fully understand the antioxidant and pro-oxidant nature of vitamin C,' Leeuwenburgh concluded" (*Free Radical Biology and Medicine*, 2001; 31 (6): 745–53).

Dr. Leeuwenburgh told me that some prominent researchers would not be happy with his study, but he said "[O]ur conditions are relevant and both unique; three factors occurring simultaneously; iron, vitamin C, oxidants, and therefore creating a physiological pro-oxidant environment." These conditions are typical of any posttraining/exercise environment within muscle tissue (e-mail to the author, 10/7/2001).

PREVENTION OF EXERCISE-INDUCED MUSCLE DAMAGE

It's common practice among athletes to megadose with supplements that claim antioxidant properties to combat excessive tissue damage after intense training sessions or when starting a new or unfamiliar routine. Some believe it will minimize "free radical damage" to muscle cell membranes. However, this effect has not been demonstrated scientifically and is, at best, only speculation.

Moreover, if the claims for antioxidants were true, they would be objectively measurable. Simply have two groups of athletes follow the same training regimen for a period of, say, eight to twelve weeks. Give one group a placebo and the other the antioxidants. If the claim is accurate, the group that receives the antioxidants will demonstrate significantly greater changes in measurements of performance and in lean body mass because of reduced levels of muscle damage and quicker recovery rates between intense sessions of exercise. This kind of result has never been demonstrated, though some have tried.

In one 2002 study, supplemental vitamin E was given thirty days prior to and one week after arm muscle soreness was induced in the subjects. The individuals who received the vitamin E experienced the same amount of muscle soreness as the placebo group (*Med Sci Sports Exerc* 2002; 34 (10): 1,605–1,613).

The same journal reported on a comparable 2002 study using twenty-year-old men who consumed either a placebo or 1,200 IU (approximately 800 mg of biologically active vitamin E) of vitamin E for thirty days prior to beginning a resistance exercise program. The study "sought to determine the effect of vitamin E on muscle damage or soreness resulting from contractions, or resistance exercise" of exhaustive knee flexion and extension contractions. When tissue was extracted by muscle biopsy and examined, researchers determined that the vitamin E supplement group did not demonstrate any decrease in cell damage or improved function over the placebo group (ACSM News Release, May 23, 2002). The report further stated that "the researchers believe that supplementation with vitamin E would not confer a protective effect over a long period of time."

Bear in mind that free radicals might actually play a mediating role in muscle adaptation to training. Considering the potential long-term harm attached to taking large doses of supplements, it is unwise and unwarranted to follow that type of regimen until the data are clear. Until then, this kind of supplementing simply becomes another unnecessary mental crutch for training, one that could actually impair recovery rates in some cases by promoting free radical production.

In 2003 the *European Journal of Applied Physiology* (89: 393–400) reported on the effects of postexercise vitamin C supplementation and recovery from demanding exercise. This study, conducted by the Department of Sport and Exercise Science at the University of Bath, demonstrated that subjects who received 400 mg/day of vitamin C after an unaccustomed bout of exercise experienced increased muscle soreness and slightly higher plasma lymphocyte (cells produced by the immune system) concentrations compared to those subjects who received a placebo.

In August 2004, the *Medicine and Science in Sports and Exercise* published the results of a study conducted on elite triathletes who were competing in the Kona World Championships. Thirty-eight triathletes ingested either 800 IU of vitamin E or a placebo for 2 months prior to the competition. Blood, urine, and saliva samples were collected the day before the race, 5–10 minutes postrace, and 1.5 hours postrace. The authors concluded that the "data indicate that vitamin E (800 IU) per day for 2 months compared with placebo ingestion before a competitive triathlon race event promotes lipid peroxidation and inflammation during exercise" (*Med Sci Sports Exerc* 2004; 36 (8): 1328–1335).

Credible researchers, including Christiaan Leeuwenburgh of the University of Florida, believe that increased muscle tissue damage may be related to three specific factors occurring simultaneously:

- the presence of unbound or free iron,
- supplemental vitamin C, and
- oxidants, or free radicals.

The excess iron can result from supplemental vitamin C, which releases iron from storage, and from iron being released from within muscle tissue cells after being damaged from exercise. The presence of free radicals is simply one physiological consequence of exercise; on their own, these free radicals would have no significant negative impact.

Additionally, Dr. Leeuwenburgh has pointed out that all antioxidant supplements are capsulated to prevent oxidation but they can certainly become oxidized and degrade into weak free radicals themselves (phone conversation with the author, 10/8/01). His point is, as Dr. Herbert's comments earlier in this chapter also pointed out, vitamin C biochemistry allows it to fluctuate between its pro-oxidant form or its antioxidant form. Unless you have the capability of testing the samples of vitamin C you purchase as a supplement, how do you know which form is present and in what quantities?

Consumers must keep in mind the three mechanisms of nutrient homeostasis, discussed in detail in Chapter 3: nutrient storage capacity, changes in nutrient absorption rates, and changes in nutrient retention or excretion rates. Consider the following research findings published in the March 2003 *Journal of Nutrition*. The authors reported that seventy-seven healthy men, age twenty to fifty-one, whose typical diet contained only an average of 2.6 servings per day of fruits and vegetables, did *not* benefit from supplemental antioxidants. Supplemental vitamins C and E did increase plasma levels, but they "had no effect on the oxidant biomarkers." The authors concluded that "the endogenous [developing from within the body] antioxidant defense system and a modest intake of dietary antioxidants are adequate to minimize levels of oxidative damage" (*J Nutr* 2003; 133: 740–743).

These individuals probably experienced increased absorption rates for what nutrients were available, as well as improved recycling of these nutrients. These mechanisms appear to be enhanced in athletes; when oxidative stress is increased, as it is with exercise, the body's antioxidant defenses are stimulated to increase as well.

One important study involved thirty-nine competitive triathletes (twenty-six men, thirteen women) who took part in the 1994 Hawaii Ironman World Championship Triathlon. This grueling event consists of a 2.4-mile swim, a 112-mile bike ride, and a 26-mile run. The study, published in the *Journal of the American Medical Association* in 1996, was intended to determine the effect of a single bout of ultraendurance exercise on the oxidative susceptibility of lipids in highly trained athletes. Among the subjects researchers found a reduced risk of "the susceptibility of lipids to peroxidation." The results, they said, appeared to be independent of antioxidant supplement use and "may be mediated by induction of endogenous antioxidants." In simpler terms, as training progresses, well-trained athletes develop an enhanced antioxidant capacity to accommodate their body's needs. (Vol. 276, No. 3, July 17, 1996)

Another study, published in the *European Journal of Applied Physiology and Occupational Physiology* (abstract 81; 1–2: 67–74), tested the hypothesis that short-term endurance exercise training would rapidly (within five days) improve the diaphragm, a muscle used to aid breathing located beneath the lungs, antioxidant capacity and would protect the diaphragm against oxidative stress. The researchers found that "biochemical analysis revealed that exercise training increased diaphragm oxidative and antioxidant capacity" from 10 percent to 24 percent, depending on the molecule measured. Their conclusion: "[T]hese data indicate that short-term exercise training can rapidly elevate oxidative capacity as well as enzymatic and non-enzymatic antioxidant defenses." Again, in simpler terms, training induces changes that enable athletes to maintain an elevated antioxidant system, which corresponds to the body's level of need, within reason.

In 2001 researchers examined "nine habitually active males who consumed a 1 gram dose of vitamin C 2 hours before exercise and on another occasion consumed an identical placebo" (*Int J Sports Med* 2001; 22: 68–75). The exercise comprised a "90 minute intermittent shuttle-running test, which was designed to stimulate the multiple-sprints sports." The test results for both trials illustrated no differences in muscle soreness, damage, or increased lipid peroxidation between the vitamin C group and the placebo group.

Another study measured blood antioxidants in twenty runners and six sedentary individuals, all twenty- to forty-year-old males. The researchers looked for correlations "between antioxidants in blood and (1) weekly training distance and (2) maximum oxygen uptake" (Robertson, J.D., et al., *Clin Sci* 1992; 82 (1): 117–118). The results indicated that vitamin E concentration in the red blood cells, as well as the antioxidant enzymes glutathione peroxidase and catalase, were "significantly and positively correlated with the weekly training distance." In addition, the study demonstrated that vitamin C concentration in the white blood cells "was significantly elevated in the high-training group."

These same antioxidant enzymes were investigated in fifteen- to twenty-one-year-old swimmers to determine their changes with training. The authors concluded "that both long-distance and particularly short-distance (100 m) swimmers increased the activities of the antioxidant defense enzymes" (*Med Sci Sports Exer* 33 (4): 564–567, April 2001).

Published reviews of the scientific literature in 2001 and 2003 in this area reached the same conclusions as the studies cited above. One review concluded that acute exercise might increase the oxidative stress in untrained muscles but that "long term exercise may counter this effect by increasing the activity of antioxidant enzymes and reducing oxidant production" (*Current Medicinal Chemistry*, 2001; 8: 829–838). The second review of the literature investigating the requirement for vitamin C with exercise concluded that "exercise does not increase the requirement for vitamin C in athletes" (*International Journal of Sport Nutrition & Exercise Metabolism*, 2003; 13 (2):). Without these critical adaptations, chronic oxidative damage, not only to the muscle tissue but also to other tissue, would result.

Finally, an interesting research paper published in 2002 in the *Journal of Nutrition* described a study that tested the effects of supplemental vitamin C on racing greyhounds. Dogs given supplements of 1 gram of vitamin C ran an average .2 seconds slower, which, according to the authors, would be equivalent to a distance of 3 meters at the finish of a 500-meter race. The authors also stated that past research on greyhounds showed that a high daily dose of vitamin E (1,000 IU) also negatively affected their speed. "[I]t is possible, therefore," they wrote, "that vitamin C was reducing performance in these greyhounds either by acting as a pro-oxidant and increasing tissue damage or by interfering with force production within muscle" (*J Nutr*, 2002; 132: 1,616s–1,621s). Although this study cannot be directly correlated to humans, the negative effects of supplemental vitamin C and E on muscle fibers is interesting and should be considered by anyone considering these supplements for the purposes of preventing muscle damage.

ENHANCED IMMUNITY IN ATHLETES

A common belief among athletes is that intense training lowers their resistance to viral and bacterial infections, particularly upper respiratory infections. It is true that overtraining—but not necessarily intense training—can play an indirect role in lessening the body's immunity. Nevertheless, and perhaps more important, overtraining is also associated with:

- lack of appetite resulting in decreased carbohydrate and caloric intake,
- lack of sleep, and
- excessive weight loss.

These factors also contribute to decreased immunity, and they play a far more significant role in immunity and overall health than the need for antioxidants. Consider these comments from the Joint Position Statement on Nutrition and Athletic Performance published by the American College of Sports Medicine, the American Dietetic Association, and Dietitians of Canada in 2000: "[A]lthough there is some evidence that acute exercise may increase levels of lipid peroxide by-products, habitual exercise has been shown to result in an augmented antioxidant system and a reduction of lipid peroxidation. *Thus, a well-trained athlete may have a more developed endogenous antioxidant system than a sedentary person*" [my emphasis]. This explains why, anecdotally, individuals who routinely exercise have fewer absentee days from work due to illness than those who do not.

Athletes who do not overtrain will tell you they are rarely ill. Their reports are consistent with studies that demonstrate athletes' and nonathletes' resting immune functions to be similar and that exercise actually enhances immunity rather than diminishing it. Specifically, a study published in the April 2004 *British Journal of Sports Medicine* reported on the "rapid and substantial" response of the immune systems of fourteen- to eighteen-year-old wrestlers after a ninety-minute wrestling practice.

Expert Input

David Nieman, DrPH, FACSM, Department of Health and Exercise Science, Appalachian State University, Boone, North Carolina, writing in a report for the Gatorade Sports Science Institute.

"Even when significant changes in concentrations and functional activities of immune variables have been observed in athletes, investigators have had little success in linking these changes to a higher incidence of infection and illness."

According to Dr. Nieman, the data do suggest "that the immune system is suppressed and stressed, albeit transiently[,] following prolonged endurance exercise. Thus, it makes sense (but still remains unproven) that upper respiratory infection rates would be increased when endurance athletes undergo repeated cycles of heavy exertion, are exposed to novel pathogens, and experience other stressors to the immune system, including lack of sleep, severe mental stress, malnutrition, or weight loss."

Dr. Nieman's work has shown no alteration of the immune response to 2.5 hours of intense running in subjects who took 1,000 mg of vitamin C daily for eight days. He also points out that "the most impressive results have been reported in the carbohydrate supplementation studies." Taking note of the correlation among various hormones, concentration of glucose in plasma, and the immune response, he states that the link is negatively affected by prolonged and intense exercise. If the intake of carbohydrate is also significantly decreased, the door is open to decreased immunity, caused both by the negative changes in hormonal balance and glucose availability as a fuel source for lymphocytes and monocytes. However, when carbohydrate intake is sufficient to meet energy demands, the situation is favorable to maintaining optimal immune function. Significantly decreased amounts of glucose—common in overtrained distance athletes—can "have a direct effect in lowering proliferation rates of lymphocytes" (meaning, more simply, that your immune system goes from a rapid response time to a slow response time).

Regarding his research, Dr. Nieman further states: "[O]overall, the hormonal and immune responses to carbohydrate ingestion, compared to placebo ingestion, suggests that physiological stress was diminished." Thus, elite athletes are less likely to have decreased immunity if they take in carbohydrates before, during, and after exercise and do not concern themselves with antioxidant supplements.

Dr. Nieman's work illustrates that the immune system must be in balance, or homeostatic equilibrium, to function properly. If this balance is disrupted, the system cannot maintain its optimal immunoprotective role. Dr. Nieman's research demonstrates that the addition of antioxidants to the diet does not diminish the incidence of infection and illness in healthy athletes and consumers, and that the immune cells responsible for eliminating pathogens have reduced proliferation rates or response to pathogens in individuals who are not consuming sufficient carbohydrates to meet their needs. Dr. Nieman's view is supported by some recent research that illustrated that "ingesting carbohydrate beverages during heavy exercise is associated with smaller changes in plasma concentrations of several cytokines." Cytokines are key regulators of the bodies' response to injury and infection; the reduced response indicates a reduced stress on the immune system. The same issue of this journal reported that preexercise carbohydrate intake could positively affect neutrophil (white blood cells) response to prolonged cycling (Bishop, N. et al. *International Journal of Sport Nutrition & Exercise Metabolism*, 11 (4), 2001).

Thus, it is clear that supplemental antioxidants do not enhance immunity and that, if you make even a reasonable effort to eat well, your body's well-designed nutrient homeostasis mechanisms provide all the support you need to maintain more than sufficient levels of necessary antioxidants and related nutrients.

So what, if anything, can supplemental antioxidants do for you? Consider some points made by Victor Herbert, MD, in a letter to the editor published in the *American Journal of Clinical Nutrition* in 1997.

Expert Input

Victor Herbert, MD, in a letter to the editor in the *American Journal of Clinical Nutrition* 1997; 65:1,901 June).

Portions of a commentary entitled "Destroying Immune Homeostasis in Normal Adults with Antioxidant Supplements."

An immune system that is in balance, or homeostatic equilibrium, is synonymous with good health. Too much or too little stimulation of the immune system can be harmful. An uncalled-for stimulation of the immune system, such as with supplemental vitamin E, can have a significant harmful immunopotentiation effect [an unnecessary or excessive immune stimulating effect]. Specifically, Dr. Herbert points out that lymphocytes [white blood cells] are equipped to eradicate noxious agents (microbes, cancer cells, and grafts [a tissue or organ transplant]) that disturb the body's equilibrium, but when lymphocyte cellular activity is excessive, the results are harmful: the same killer lymphocytes that are immunoprotective can be immunopathogenic. What role they take on in is determined to a significant extent by the orderliness or derangements of lymphocyte programmed cell death (apoptosis), the physiological process essential to normal cell development and homeostasis. In other words, the lymphocytes' programmed function and life span (orderliness) is precise enough to enable them to respond to any foreign antigen in the body, destroy it, and then die themselves to prevent excessive tissue damage. If this process is negatively modified (derangement) then the lymphocytes are capable of destroying healthy tissue. Dr. Herbert points out the concern that if normal physiological processes do not curtail the activity of T cells (immune cells that respond to foreign substances when they enter your body) when their usefulness has ended, these cells can continue to attack healthy tissue without interference, which is referred to as immunopathogenic—an obvious negative effect.

According to Dr. Herbert, further research needs to be done to determine whether vitamin E, particularly dl-alpha tocopherol (the dominant vitamin E in supplements) not only stimulates T cell production, but also triggers inhibition of programmed cell death of the T cells it generates.

Finally, Dr. Herbert states that the lucrative vitamin C, vitamin E, and other "immune enhancers" of the supplement industry may harm millions by not labeling their products, "Caution, this product's immune enhancement may be bad for you."

A study published in the *Journal of the American Medical Association* in 2002 supported Dr. Herbert's position. This study followed 650 well-nourished, noninstitutionalized elderly individuals in the Netherlands for two years to investigate the effect of daily multivitamin-mineral and vitamin E supplementation on acute respiratory tract infections. The subjects were divided into four groups: a placebo group, a multivitamin group, a vitamin E group, and a multivitamin and vitamin E group. Individuals who received 200 mg of vitamin E per day experienced significantly more symptoms and were ill five days longer than the placebo group. The study showed no favorable advantage in receiving the multivitamins and minerals over the placebo group (*JAMA* 2002; 288; 715–721).

The September 23, 2002, *Nutrition News Focus* newsletter commented on the study, pointing out the need for a balance of free radical production in order to maintain health. The article stated, "[I]t is not known why those taking vitamin E were sicker, but white blood cells kill invading viruses and bacteria by generating free radicals. This is one time you do not want too many antioxidants in your system." Nevertheless, what is the first response by millions of Americans who feel they are "coming down with a cold"? They take large doses of vitamin C.

A study testing the administration of vitamin E and beta-carotene or a placebo on men fifty to sixty-nine years old performing heavy exercise suggested that "vitamin E and beta-carotene increased the risk of colds in subjects carrying out heavy exercise at leisure" (*Med Sci Sports Exerc* 2003; 35 (11): 1815–1820).

The Bottom Line

I believe that the scientific data available at this time does not support the use of antioxidant supplements by athletes or non-athletic consumers to increase recovery time, to prevent excessive tissue breakdown from free radical production, or to enhance the immune system after intense training and competition or in general. In fact, they may actually hinder training and development. Popping some pills simply cannot eliminate the negative consequences of a poorly planned training program that results in overtraining. It would be far wiser to develop a solid, progressive conditioning program with the necessary adequate rest and to significantly increase the intake of fruits, vegetables, grains, nuts, and beans, to accommodate the additional training intensity or time. Remember that vitamin C, vitamin E, and beta-carotene make up only a small percentage of the nutrients actually available from foods. The long-term safety of high doses of the purported antioxidants is questionable at best and possibly dangerous for some. Athletes should know they might run the risk of making the tissue stress of excessive training worse by taking supplemental antioxidants.

Research clearly shows that a key to maintaining a highly responsive immune system is to prevent overtraining and its consequences: excessive weight loss in a short period, lack of appetite and the resulting negative effects of reduced carbohydrate intake, and lack of rest. These factors have a direct role in maintaining both health and a competitive edge, but they typically are overlooked—or ignored—by those who have the mental capability to motivate themselves beyond what the body is capable of adapting to over short periods. This is a persistent problem for many athletes and active consumers.

As for those upper respiratory infections, it is likely that many athletes do experience increased viral infections after intense competition, simply because they have gone from independent training sessions to competition, where they are likely to be exposed to others who might be carrying pathogens.

Scientists are concerned about the effects of indiscriminate dosing with vitamins that have antioxidant capabilities, particularly since the body appears to be capable of increasing its own antioxidant production when needed. However, many professionals and educators who advise athletes are swayed by the opinions of supplement company's representatives. Sometimes these opinions even find their way into the scholarly literature. A report entitled "Free Radicals, Exercise, and Antioxidants" that appeared in 1999 in the peer-reviewed technical journal for the National Strength and Conditioning Association contained the following statements:

- Almost no toxicity or adverse effects have been reported with oral administration of vitamin E in any form in doses up to 1,600 mg/day.
- A consensus on reviews has shown complete safety with dosages of vitamin C of 1 to 5 g/day.
- Beta-carotene has been shown to be safe at any dose.

The only problem is, as I have illustrated in this chapter, these statements are blatantly false! The combination of a well planned training program, which results in a positive adaptation of skeletal muscle antioxidant capacity, as well as a good diet providing the necessary phytochemicals which synergistically work together, is all most athletes need.

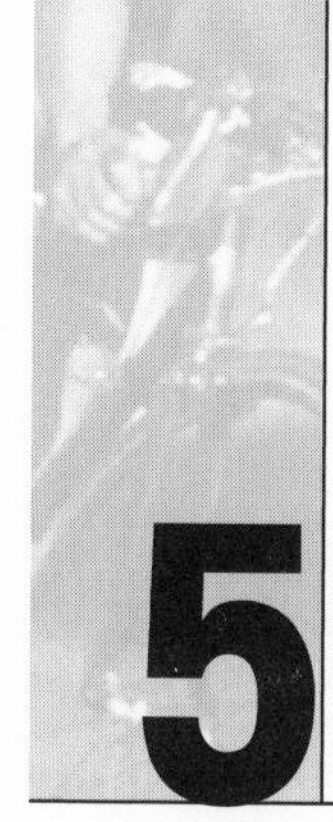

5 PROTEIN AND MUSCLE MASS

HOW MUCH IS ENOUGH?

Everybody knows muscle is mostly protein. Everybody also knows that a lot of extra protein is required to build muscle and keep it healthy. Right? Well, actually, it's not.

"Everybody" is wrong.

Similarly, most people believe that muscle is anywhere from 75 percent to 100 percent protein. In fact, muscle is roughly 70 percent water! It contains only about 22 percent protein. Stop here a moment, and do the math. Let's say you want to add a pound of muscle to your current body weight per week. If a pound of muscle contains 22 percent protein, how many grams of protein must you consume beyond your normal diet to achieve this goal?

22 percent of one pound (454 grams) = roughly 100 grams

If one pound of muscle contains roughly 100 grams of protein, how many extra grams of protein will be you need to consume per day?

100 grams/7 days = 14.3 grams per day

What can you consume to add approximately 15 grams of protein to your daily diet?

- 2 cups nonfat milk (18 g), or
- 2 cups rice and beans (18 g), or
- 3 ounces chicken (21 g)

Most people are amazed at how easy it is to boost the protein in their diet simply by adding what amounts to a healthy snack! In fact, I have looked at hundreds of five-day diet histories, and it is rare for athletes, unless they are strict vegetarians or consuming too few total calories, to be deficient in protein. Nevertheless, supplement companies are making millions selling protein supplements.

Supplement manufacturers also exaggerate the *amount* of muscle mass that can be developed with the aid of protein supplements. Even with continual strenuous physical exercise, big muscle gains after the first few years of strength training are not likely for most people. Each year after the initial two years of weight training, the developmental rate slows to half—or less—of what it was to the point that development progresses at a snail's pace or stops completely, when genetic limitations are achieved and muscle maintenance begins. On top of that, gains in muscle mass vary greatly due to many factors, including genetics, gender, rest, diet, age, and type of training.

> *Expert Input*
>
> **Steven J. Fleck, PhD, and William J. Kraemer, PhD, in *Designing Resistance Training Programs*:**
>
> "The largest increases in lean body mass are a little greater than 3 kilograms (6.6 lb) in 10 weeks of training. This translates into a lean body mass of 0.66 pounds per week. Though some coaches desire huge gains in body weight for their athletes during the off-season, this is impossible if that added body weight is going to be muscle mass."

Once you have a basic understanding of both the possibilities and limitations of muscle development, a mental "quack alarm" should sound as soon as you hear about a way to gain two to three pounds per week of solid muscle. You're obviously dealing with someone uneducated in muscle physiology and nutrition, someone who'll stretch the truth to make money, or, more charitably, someone who has misinterpreted gains in fat mass, bone mass, increased water retention, or increased stored sugar as muscle mass development.

In 1995 supplement manufacturer Met-Rx sent to my office an unpublished "study" entitled "Met-Rx Substantiation Report of October 1993." According to the report, a number of Dallas Cowboys made tremendous gains during a six-week period of using the company's nutritional mix. A defensive end was purported to have gained 15 pounds of muscle, an offensive lineman 19 pounds of muscle, and an offensive tackle 14 pounds of "solid new muscle." Even for a professional athlete, and even for someone taking an anabolic-androgenic steroid as opposed to a supplement, a gain of 2.3 to 3.2 pounds of solid new muscle per week would be phenomenal.

> *Expert Input*
>
> **Karl Friedl, PhD, in *Anabolic Steroids in Sport and Exercise*, edited by Charles Yesalis, PhD:**
>
> "The majority of short-term studies (3–10 weeks) result in 3–5 kg of body weight gain . . . the upper limit is around 20 kg (44 pounds) of lean mass" [over a couple of years of use].

Initial results reported in steroid studies are 3 to 5 kg (6.6 lbs to 11 lbs) gain of muscle mass, equivalent to 1.1 pounds per week over a ten-week period. How likely is it that an overpriced protein drink will provide twice the results of steroids? If these protein supplements worked as well as their advertisers claim, it would be easy to validate the claims with a few well-controlled double-blind, peer-reviewed studies, but this has never happened.

Incidentally, the March 13, 2006 *Sports Illustrated* article on Barry Bonds and steroids reported that Bonds purportedly gained "15 pounds of muscle in 100 days" (pg. 42). This would be equivalent to .95 pounds per week, which would be consistent with steroid use and not some ineffective protein concoction. The figures provided are accurate.

Recall from Chapter 2 the implied claim of increased muscle mass development with the use of the Weider product Anabolic Mega-Pak. The product name itself implies muscle enhancement beyond that which a normal diet can provide. Such results should be observable in well-controlled studies, but Weider was unable to provide satisfactory documentation of its claims to the FTC in 1984, resulting in the company having to put the following disclaimer on the back of the product: "As with all supplements, use of this product *will not promote* [my emphasis] faster or greater muscular gains. This product is, however a nutritious low-fat food supplement which, like other foods, provides nutritional support for weight training athletes."

Muscle physiology is very efficient, enabling us to walk great distances and work long, physically challenging hours while still having the strength to perform other necessary tasks. If our bodies actually needed the enormous protein intake promoted by supplement manufacturers, there would be significant muscle wasting in athletes and blue-collar workers who do not consume high-protein diets or take protein supplements. However, research has consistently shown that athletes and adults who do physically hard work need no more than 1.2 to 2.0 grams of protein daily per kilogram of body weight—an intake that is easily accomplished with wise food choices.

By design, muscle tissue is most efficient when it utilizes carbohydrates and fats for energy. Protein is an inefficient energy source, because it is not used by the body in the same form in which it is consumed. First, the liver must remove the nitrogen molecule (which is excreted in the urine) before it breaks down, or hydrolyzes, the rest of the carbon skeleton of protein and converts it to glucose. Only then can it be burned as fuel. And only when there is significantly diminished glucose and fat fuel sources would protein play any significant role as fuel. When the excess protein consumed by supplement users is broken down, the excess nitrogen can cause a change in urine color (the nitrogen makes urine a darker yellow) and an increase in urination frequency. The resulting fluid loss could play a role in inducing dehydration, which has the capacity to significantly impede performance, as discussed in Chapter 6.

> *Expert Input*
>
> **Peter Lemon, PhD, in the *International Journal of Sports Nutrition,* 1998; 8: 426–447.**
>
> There can be a "four to fivefold increase in urine volume" in some individuals consuming excessive protein intakes (greater than 2.0 g per 2.2 lb body weight)."

Researchers at the University of Connecticut's Department of Nutritional Sciences who studied hydration levels in athletes presented their findings at the April 2002 meeting of the Federation of American Societies for Experimental Biology. The researchers provided athletes with either 68 grams, 123 grams, or 246 grams of protein daily for four weeks. Those athletes consuming the greatest amounts of protein demonstrated significantly lower hydration levels (Web MD Medical News, April 22, 2002 "High Protein Diets Cause Dehydration," by Liza Maltin) (http://www.webmd.com/content/article/24/2731_1705.htm.)

Why Do Consumers Believe They Need Protein Supplements?

Many athletes and other individuals taking protein supplements do believe they are effective—and some are actually seeing results. There are four main reasons why protein supplements can seem to be effective:

- the placebo effect,
- natural progression,
- stimulants, and
- a carbohydrate deficient diet.

PLACEBO EFFECT

When real expectations accompany the use of a product that promises certain mental or physical enhancements, there can be a significant improvement in performance. These changes, however, are unrelated to any actual biological effects of the product. It's simply the placebo effect, the mental transformation of expectations into real gains.

A 1972 study of male varsity athletes provides a perfect example of the placebo effect. The intent of the study was to measure improvement in performance among well-trained athletes who expected to make gains while on steroids. The athletes had undergone two years of hard weight training for five days a week (twice a week during vacations). The study measured their improvements at the seated military press, bench press, curls, and squats.

According to Gideon Ariel, PhD, who reported on the study in the *American College of Sports Medicine Journal* in 1972 the athletes "were informed that some of them would be selected to receive an anabolic steroid (Dianabol). Instead, six selected subjects were given placebo pills. . . . When the total progress in all four exercises for the two periods was tested, the subjects had a significant improvement during both periods. When these gains were compared, a significant difference was evident in favor of the placebo period" (Vol. 4, Issue 2: 124–126). Taking the placebo apparently supplied the psychological benefits the athletes needed to obtain strength gains beyond those that would be expected from a reasonable progression of their athletic activity. The placebo effect is very real and powerful, and it is a dominant factor in explaining why many athletes develop a misplaced faith in supplements. Prominent athletes who make sales pitches for certain supplement products are, all too often, testifying based on their own experience with the placebo effect.

NATURAL PROGRESSION

It's a simple concept: consistent, well-planned training produces changes in skills and strength levels. When athletes take an inert product around the same time they would see natural progression in physical development due to training, they tend to credit the product instead of the training.

STIMULANTS

Some supplement products contain stimulants, such as ephedrine (now off the market), synephrine or bitter orange (which has replaced ephedrine in many products), or caffeine, that may or may not appear on the ingredient list. When they are taken prior to any mental or physical challenge, the effect of stimulants on the central nervous system can provide a significant increase in mental focus and energy level. However, these stimulants are not without dangers. Recall the twenty-three-year-old male I mentioned in Chapter 2, for whom I conducted a preemployment strength and biomechanics screening. The young man, a body builder, used a product which contained the stimulants ephedrine and caffeine, resulting in a blood pressure of 280/120 and a heart rate of 110 bpm. This young man's energy level was obviously high, and his ability to lift in the gym probably was intense. Yet his potential for a cardiovascular disaster was very real, given the combination of a very high resting blood pressure and the additional increased blood pressure that would occur from lifting heavy weights.

A CARBOHYDRATE-DEFICIENT DIET

A diet low in carbohydrates is not unusual among adults, even among athletes. In individuals with deficient carbohydrate intake, intense physical labor or training can chronically diminish or exhaust the energy stores of carbohydrate. The result is fatigue, poor physical performance, and limited strength development. Repeatedly, I have observed weekly work output and strength gains in athletes who have simply begun to consume more carbohydrates on a daily basis.

Let's say that a given athlete's energy demands on Monday through Friday are 400 calories per day greater than his current calorie intake. Performances at Monday and Tuesday practices are fine, but starting Wednesday his energy and performance diminish earlier and earlier in the practice session. Because the athlete starts each session with less and less carbohydrate in storage, he cannot maintain the intensity of the workout. However, if he consumes a protein drink that contains some carbohydrate, or a related supplement that provides calories, he will probably experience an improvement in energy level and performance. His tendency will be to credit the improvement to the protein (or some other ingredient) in the drink or supplement. The truth is that he would have maintained or even improved energy and performance much more efficiently by making good food choices to provide him adequate carbohydrates throughout the week.

To illustrate just how important sufficient carbohydrate intake is for the development of muscle mass, consider some points made by Karl Friedl, PhD, in *Anabolic Steroids in Sport and Exercise*, edited by Charles Yesalis, PhD. According to Dr. Friedl, insufficient energy intake relative to energy needs "may be one of the principal causes of decreased testosterone in sustained exercise events where it may be difficult to maintain energy balance" (pg. 161). Dr. Friedl states that this decrease in testosterone is believed to be a function of the hypothalamus of the brain; the hypothalamus detects that there are insufficient calories to sustain current muscle mass and therefore inhibits any new muscle mass development. (This mechanism is very similar to the "false athletic anorexia" observed in many female athletes and discussed in Chapter 7.)

Dr. Friedl states that inadequate energy intake will result in a decline in thyroid hormones and testosterone, which in turn would favor the "loss of fast-twitch (type II) muscle fibers and would be unfavorable to strength athletes" (pg. 161) as well as those involved in sprinting or jumping sports.

If Protein Supplements Don't Work, Then How Do Those Guys Get So Big?

On average, athletes are bigger and stronger today than they were two to three decades ago. The primary reasons for this are fairly simple:

- better understanding of muscle physiology and biochemistry;
- year-round training and conditioning programs, starting as early as high school;
- better equipment, injury prevention, and rehabilitation programs;
- better nutrition for some; and
- steroid use by many.

These five factors have made a very real impact on the physical development of many male and female athletes. For example, in the physical therapy practice where I work, a newspaper article from a 1957 junior college football game includes the heights and weights of the starting players on both teams, one of which was ranked third nationally. The average offensive line weight was 199 pounds for one team and 194.5 for the other. Only five players weighed more than 200 pounds. By today's standards, these stats might fit a small high school varsity team.

However, these factors *cannot* explain the major changes in muscular and skeletal development of a significant growing contingent of athletes and "health" enthusiasts. There is only one explanation for the way these individuals, both professionals and amateurs, have greatly surpassed what their late-teen and early-twenties physiques indicated they would be capable of achieving: steroids.

The normal adult male naturally produces 35 to 50 mg per week of testosterone. Typical steroid users inject up to 1,000 mg, twenty times their normal levels, over the same time period.

Consider the following information from *Anabolic Steroids in Sport and Exercise*:

> *"It is absolutely rampant right now," says one American League front office executive, who talked only on condition his name would not be used. "But baseball doesn't care. The Players Association does not care. The owners don't care."*
>
> *"Steroids have completely changed the game. Guys try to cover it up by saying they're using creatine. Or they're just lifting weights now. Come on. It's a completely different look. I can pick out a kid using creatine from a kid on 'roids.*
>
> *"Go ahead and get pictures of guys when they were 22 years old, and look at them now. Look at their faces. Look at the size of their heads now. That's not creatine."*
>
> *—Ken Rosenthal*

> *"People who get caught are either badly managed or have very stupid doctors."*
>
> *—Anonymous British sportsman*

> *"Far and away the most frequently occurring side effect of using steroids is that you become a liar."*
>
> *—Anonymous bodybuilder, quoted by*
> *Peter Hildreth, OP/ED* London Times,
> *August 23, 1999*

"Anabolic steroid's biggest side effect is loss of memory because no one can remember taking them."

—Anonymous All-Pro lineman

"Americans like to think the U.S. leads the 'Sports without Drugs Crusade,' but 'the reality is that the U.S. is viewed as one of the dirtiest nations in the world,' says Roger Ruger, past chair of the United States Olympic Committee Athletes' Advisory Council."

—"Mass Deception: Today's Athlete Is Getting Bigger, Stronger, Faster . . . Unnaturally," Sport, *August 1998*

In 1987 only 27 NFL players weighed more than 300 pounds, while in 1997 there were approximately 240 players over 300 pounds. Some argue that the size increases is a consequence of high-calorie diets and food supplements such as creatine, while others point their finger at anabolic steroids and human growth hormone (hGH) as the cause.

After winning in the 1971 Pan American games in Cali, Colombia, weightlifter Ken Patera relished meeting Russian Superheavyweight Vasily Alexeyev in the 1972 Olympics in Munich. Patera was quoted in the Los Angeles Times*:*

"Last year the only difference between him and me was I couldn't afford his drug bill. Now I can. When I hit Munich I'll weigh in at about 340, or maybe 350. Then we'll see which are better, his steroids or mine."

After a lengthy investigation of drug use in Olympic sports, Bamberger and Yaeger (1997) concluded that: Three distinct classes of top-level athletes have emerged in many Olympic sports. One is a small group of athletes who are not using any banned performance enhancers. The second is a large, burgeoning group whose drug use goes undetected; these athletes either take drugs

> *that aren't tested for, use tested-for drugs in amounts below the generous levels permitted by the IOC or take substances that mask the presence of the drugs in their system at testing time. The third group comprises the smattering of athletes who use banned performance enhancers and are actually caught.*

A 2003 article in the *Journal of Strength and Conditioning Research* reported that "the results from a survey administered to gym members in El Paso, Texas showed that steroid use was present in approximately 11% of the population surveyed" (14 (3): 289–294).

On March 12, 2004, *USA Today* reported on its investigation of steroid and drug use in professional wrestling. The report included the following observations about professional wrestlers:

1. Their death rates are about seven times higher than the general population's.
2. They are twelve times more likely to die from heart disease than are other Americans age twenty-five to forty-four.
3. They are about twenty times more likely to die before forty-five than are pro football players.
4. Some wrestlers bet among themselves about who will die next.
5. Steroids are an ingrained part of their culture.
6. An attorney for one wrestling organization stated, "[T]esting for steroids [does] not work because wrestlers can fake urine tests or use designer steroids that are undetectable." He is also reported to have stated that "anybody who wants to beat can beat it. The only ones who are caught are stupid."

According to *USA Today*, an estimated 20 million fans, including children, watch professional wrestling every week.

Of course, wrestling is not the only sport affected by steroid use. In March 2002, in the *Baseball Weekly* column "Around the Basepaths," Bob Nightengale wrote, "Scouts and executives are appalled this spring by the vast weight gains by several power hitters, believing that steroid use is rampant. An informal survey of 20 scouts, officials and players last week suggested that they believe that 65% to 70% of all players now use steroids."

On October 18, 2005 the *Washington Post* reported that 5 dietary supplements promoted on the internet for muscle development were contaminated with illegal steroids. The *Post* paid to have the UCLA Olympic Analytical Lab analyze the supplements and determined 4 of the 5 were contaminated with previously unknown designer steroids.

On March 9, 2006, the *FDA News* repeated the warning of several dietary supplement manufacturers to stop selling "unapproved drugs containing steroids" that are "promoted for building muscle and increasing strength" (www.fda.gov/bbs/topics/NEWS/2006/NEW01332.html).

Creatine and Muscle Gain

Creatine actually has some solid research which indicates that it may assist in the early physical development for some athletes. However, there are a number of issues the athlete should understand before they consider using creatine.

Like protein, creatine is a naturally occurring amino acid constructed from arginine, glycine and methionine, and is produced naturally by the body and consumed in foods, and also sold as a sports supplement. Some creatine users will notice a decrease in urine production, which indicates that the body is retaining water. Many consumers misinterpret this water retention as muscle mass development due to the increase in body weight.

This water retention may have an adverse impact on muscle tissues. Specifically, the *Clinical Journal of Sports Medicine* has reported that "creatine supplementation abnormally increases anterior compartment pressure in the lower leg at rest and following 20 minutes of level running at 80% of maximal aerobic power" in college-age males. In one study, creatine supplementation for six days resulted in increased compartment pressures 76 percent higher at rest, 150 percent higher immediately following exercise, 125 percent higher one minute postexercise, and 106 percent higher five minutes postexercise compared to a placebo group. The abnormal rise in anterior compartment pressure remained significantly higher for the creatine group compared to the placebo group after thirty-four days of creatine supplementation (*Clin J Sport Med* 2001; 11 (2): 87–95). It's reasonable to ask what other muscle groups, soft tissues, or organs' internal compartment pressures might be equally affected by creatine. What long-term effects would this increased compartment pressure have? What effects would abnormally large doses of creatine and related possible water retention have on the brain over time? Would the increase in anterior compartment pressures in the tibia make these individuals more susceptible to anterior compartment pressure syndrome (a condition that results in the compression of the nerve to the foot, which can result in reduced motor control of the foot and significant pain while running)?

These are only speculative questions, but remember that it can take many years before we realize the effect of excessive doses of any supplement on our health. To date most studies have focused on only three potential negative side effects: muscle function, heat illness, and kidney function. Creatine does not appear to negatively effect muscle function in most individuals, if they maintain good hydration, but there is anecdotal evidence that creatine users without proper hydration may experience an increased incidence of cramping, heat illness, and muscle tightness. Studies on creatine and kidney function have covered relatively short periods of use (twenty-one months or shorter); most of these studies have used biological markers to determine safety and so far have failed to illustrate any significant concern for most people. Many well qualified and respected researchers consider creatine to be safe and effective.

However, these researchers often tend to overlook additional potential problems with many creatine products when they recommend them. As an example, the authors of a study published in 1999 in the *Journal of Exercise Physiology Online* highlighted the positive changes in lean body mass, but not in strength, associated with the creatine products used (*JEPonline*, 1999, 2(2): 24–39). They make no mention of the 18 mg of iron (twice the recommended levels) and iron's potential toxicity with some males who may already genetically absorb too much. They also failed to mention the potential problems with the high chromium levels (4 times the recommended levels) or the zinc levels which may interfere with copper absorption. Considering the fact that many athletes take multiple products, it is a real possibility that many can easily acquire through excessive supplementation unhealthy dosages of zinc.

The bottom line is that no one can state objectively and with certainty that, ten to twenty years from now, creatine supplementation will have no negative long-term effects on brain or other organ functions. And, unlike steroids, creatine will not override whatever limits genetics have naturally placed on your muscle development. Creatine may assist some in reaching a particular genetic end point a little sooner but it will not take anyone beyond their natural genetic limitations. Nonusers, with a little more patience and perseverance will achieve the same goals.

Finally, since the effects of creatine on those under eighteen have not been studied, children and teenagers, who are still experiencing rapid cell division and multiplication, should not take creatine.

Consider the following statement from the Blue Cross and Blue Shield Association's Healthy Competition Foundation Position Statement on Creatine Supplementation: "The long-term effects of creatine use have not been fully examined, and to ignore the potential concerns that surround this supplement could place athletes on the path to serious health problems. Creatine is an unregulated substance that is marketed to and used in large doses by teenagers without proper medical supervision."

6 CARBOHYDRATES AND WATER

THE REAL ERGOGENIC AIDS

Whether discussing student or professional athletes, Bureau of Land Management Hotshot firefighters, or active adults simply attempting to maintain some reasonable level of conditioning, the lack of quality carbohydrates and water in the diet is without question the most prevalent problem hindering their physical development and health. Most athletes only consume 40 to 50 percent of their total calories from carbohydrates versus the recommended 55–65 percent for most. While this may seem simplistic, a shortage of carbohydrates or hydration has a broad impact, affecting the physical development, training intensity, and overall health of active consumers and athletes alike. What's more, the negative consequences of insufficient carbohydrate and water consumption increase with each additional day of training, resulting in a significantly reduced ability to perform or train by the end of each week. Most athletes and coaches misinterpret the negative consequences associated with insufficient carbohydrates and water as being the result of either lack of rest or overtraining, or a combination of the two, when in fact reduced performance is directly related to chronic poor food choices and hydration practices.

Carbohydrates

Many athletes and active consumers succumb to a wide variety of misinformation and hype regarding dietary supplements. Many are willing to try every concoction advertised—yet the same individuals who embrace these empty promises often neglect the most obvious ergogenic aid available to them by ingesting a chronically low carbohydrate or plant-based diet.

Consider the following ergogenic and health claims for Product X:

- Increases endurance and ability to maintain higher intensity levels for longer periods of time.
- Increases ability to lose excess body fat.
- May naturally increase testosterone levels.
- May increase the numbers of fast-twitch muscle fibers.
- Enhances immune function.
- Increases coordination, reaction time, and concentration and reduces likelihood of injury.
- Significantly decreases the risk of developing cancer and heart disease.

Are these the claims of the latest sport supplement? Perhaps, but they're also the actual benefits of a diet that includes sufficient quality carbohydrates. One of the greatest ironies of the supplement business is how readily most consumers are willing to purchase them and at the same time how unwilling they are to change their dietary habits. Many athletes simply neglect this area of their training, leading to any of all or the following consequences.

THE SEVEN CONSEQUENCES OF INSUFFICIENT CARBOHYDRATES

- Inability to sustain intensity levels or duration, especially by the end of a week of training
- Reduced ability to lose excess body fat
- Reduced testosterone levels
- Loss of fast-twitch muscle fibers
- Decreased immunity
- Decreased coordination, reaction time, and concentration, and increased incidence of injury
- Increased incidence of cancer and heart disease

Inability to Sustain Intensity Levels or Duration

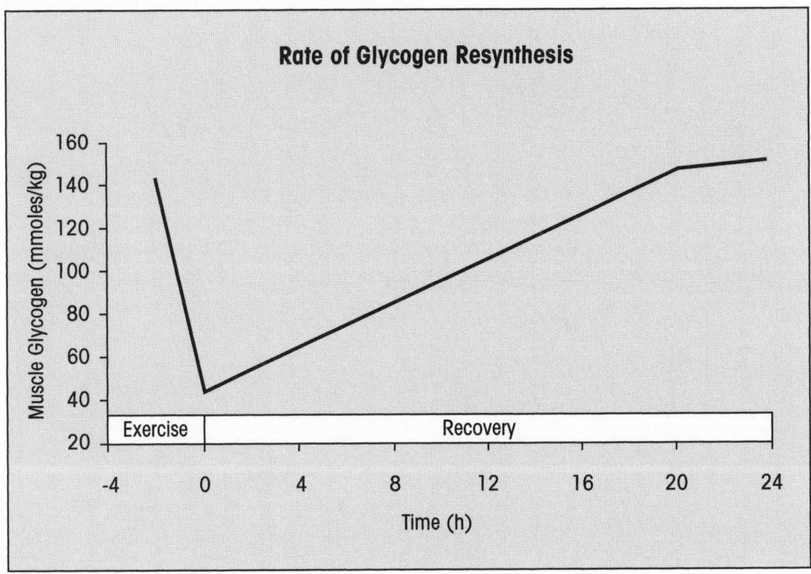

Figure 1

Figure 1 illustrates the energy cost of a typical training session. The downward sloping line on the left represents stored sugar used during the training session. This sugar utilization typically happens at a rate of 500 to 1,100 calories per hour, depending on the activity and the athlete's condition, size, age, and gender.

The upward sloping line from left to right represents the redepositing of sugar (as glycogen) back into the muscle and liver over the next twenty-four hours, *provided carbohydrate intake is sufficient,* which it typically is not and as stated, generally runs 20 to 30 percent below where the carbohydrate intake should be. This is precisely why many athletes fatigue early and why they fail to peak or to achieve specific training goals on a reasonable schedule. They simply fail to put all of the gas back into the tank, and the deficiency is exacerbated as the training week progresses.

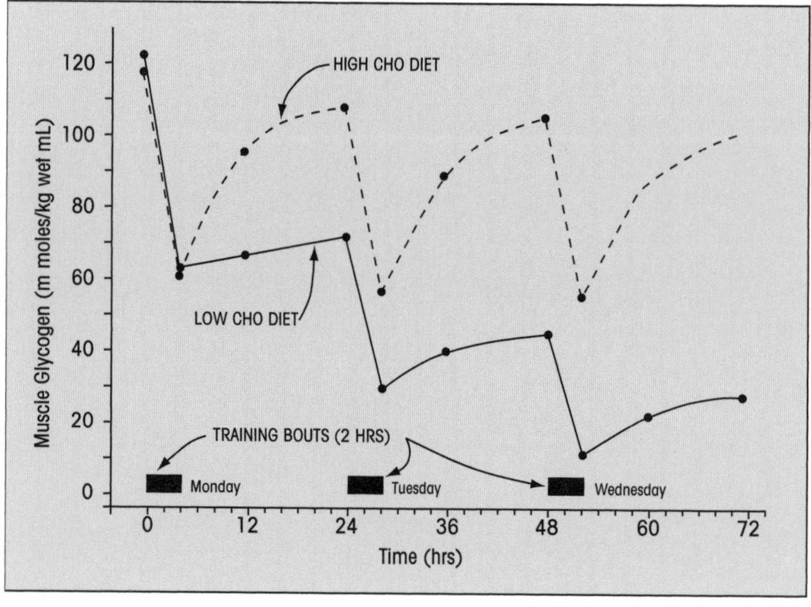

Figure 2

Figure 2 illustrates a continuation of Figure 1 through the rest of the week. The first downward sloping line again represents the amount of stored sugar utilized during the first practice of the week on Monday. Between Monday and Tuesday there are two upward sloping lines, one solid and one hatched. The solid line represents the typical diet of many athletes, with limited carbohydrate intake over the twenty-four hours following Monday's practice. The hatched line represents the amount of sugar replenishing that would have taken place if the carbohydrates in the diet had been sufficient. Clearly, those athletes consuming a higher carbohydrate diet significantly replenish their levels of muscle fuel (sugar) between practices, while those on a lower carbohydrate diet do not.

On Tuesday, both solid and hatched downward sloping lines again represent the amount of stored sugar, or glycogen, that will be used during the next practice session (day 2). Those on a lower carbohydrate diet start each successive practice with significantly less available muscle fuel (sugar), compared to those in the higher carbohydrate group.

By following the progression of the lines through Thursday and Friday, it is easy to see that those athletes who do not consume sufficient carbohydrates will have insufficient energy stores at the beginning of practice sessions later in the week. Those athletes begin to demonstrate early signs of fatigue and decreased performance by Thursday—an effect that is directly related to insufficient carbohydrate intake and not necessarily to the physical training exertion.

Simply put, athletes who consume enough carbohydrates will have significantly greater amounts of stored sugar to draw upon at the end of the week. When the end of the week arrives, these athletes will outperform an opponent who has not eaten properly.

The average person stores only about 1,500 to 2,000 calories as glycogen in the muscle, liver, and blood sugar. However, according to Paul Fournier, PhD, a researcher with the Department of Human Movement and Exercise Science at the University of Western Australia, his department's work has shown that conditioning dramatically increases this sugar storage function, reaching about 4,000 calories for some well-trained athletes. However, insufficient carbohydrate intake dramatically affects available energy by the end of the training week *regardless* of the individual's level of conditioning.

Reduced Ability to Lose Excess Body Fat

Remember that carbohydrates, or sugars, are muscle tissue's primary fuel. Muscle tissue also utilizes significant amounts of fatty acids from either stored body fat or from the diet, but how efficiently it utilizes this fat depends on the availability of sugar (carbs), how well conditioned the muscle tissue is and how long it can work comfortably at high intensity levels, such as 70 percent to 80 percent of maximum. Insufficient carbohydrate intake simply inhibits optimal fatty acid utilization.

Both of these factors are linked to the availability of carbohydrates in the diet. If carbohydrate intake is too low, muscles can only work at high intensity levels for very limited durations. This in turn prevents the development of the cellular changes necessary, which enable the muscle tissue to utilize larger and larger quantities of stored fat and fatty acids from food. The combination of decreased duration due to fatigue and decreased physiological adaptations significantly inhibit the body's fatty acid utilization. High carbohydrate intake also blunts certain hormonal changes that accompany prolonged exercise and that contribute to both central fatigue in the brain and peripheral fatigue in the muscle tissue.

The extreme popularity of low-carbohydrate diets, such as the Atkins diet, is ironic, considering that prolonged adherence to these diets will greatly inhibit the body's long-term ability to lose and maintain any significant weight loss because the low carbohydrate intake directly inhibits training duration and the normally resulting adaptations, which would have taken place.

Reduced Testosterone Levels

If carbohydrate or total energy intake is insufficient relative to training level demands, it is impossible to develop and maintain new muscle tissue. When energy intake is too low to sustain current energy demands, the brain responds by adapting. The hypothalamus may lower the levels of hormones responsible for the stimulation and development of new muscle mass, including testosterone and the thyroid hormones. Karl Friedl, PhD states "energy deficits have well-established effects mediated through the hypothalamus," which would lower testosterone levels in underfed or overtrained athletes. Karl Friedl is the research manager for the Military Operational Medicine Research Program at the U.S. Army Medical Research and Material Command in Frederick, Maryland.

Loss of Fast-Twitch Muscle Fibers

Karl Friedl, PhD, has also pointed out that as a result of reduced energy intake "the decline in thyroid hormones and testosterone favors a loss of fast-twitch (type II) muscle fibers and would be unfavorable to strength athletes" (Charles E. Yesalis, editor, *Anabolic Steroids in Sport and Exercise*, 2nd edition, pg. 161). These fibers are necessary for any explosive, agility-, or speed-related movements. The loss of a significant number of these fibers would obviously reduce performance or inhibit the appropriate improvement one would typically expect from physical training.

Decreased Immunity

The white blood cells need carbohydrates in order to proliferate normally throughout the body and aid the immune system in combating invading bacteria, viruses, and fungi. Many athletes with insufficient carb intake become ill the moment they attempt to increase the intensity or duration of their training program. In addition to the information provided in the antioxidant chapter illustrating how insufficient carbohydrate intake negatively affects immune function in athletes, researchers have demonstrated similar findings with Wildland Firefighters. Researchers at the University of Montana Human Performance Laboratory and Missoula Technology Development Center in Montana have demonstrated that the maintenance of blood glucose levels with sufficient carbohydrates intake throughout the day, positively affects the immune function of these firefighters, as well as cognitive function, mood and work output (Abstract; Eight International Wildland Fire Safety Summit, April 26–28, 2005 Missoula, MT, Brian Sharkey, PhD).

During forest fire suppression work, these individuals may be required to work twelve to twenty-four hours at higher altitude and may require 6,000 calories per day.

Decreased Coordination, Reaction Time, and Concentration, and Increased Incidence of Injury

It is common knowledge among sports scientists that the combination of central (brain) fatigue and peripheral (muscle) fatigue brought on by prolonged exercise and insufficient glucose to maintain brain and nerve tissue energy needs, significantly affects the ability to concentrate and react to external stimuli and the muscular coordination to do so. Remember, the primary fuel source for both the brain and nervous tissue is glucose (carbs). If glucose from carbs is insufficient then diminished function of both tissues will result. All these factors increase the susceptibility to injuries, especially toward the end of a training week or a lengthy competitive event. The risk of injury is even greater in contact sports, such as football, rugby, soccer, and basketball where the athlete's reaction time to those around him, changes in direction, stabilization when landing after jumping, etc. plays such a critical role in injury prevention.

Increased Incidence of Cancer and Heart Disease

It is well established that limited intake, one to three servings per day, of fruits, vegetables, cereals, and grains significantly raises the risks of developing cancer, heart disease, or other chronic health conditions. These carbohydrate foods contain thousands of various plant chemicals that play a significant role in our health. By omitting thousands of anticancer and health-promoting chemicals from their diet, individuals who consume very little of these foods substantially raise their risk factor for developing these conditions.

Unfortunately, most athletes and active consumers believe they consume sufficient quantities of carbohydrates—whether they do or not. However, five-day diet histories routinely indicate that most people's intake of necessary carbohydrate foods is significantly deficient.

Two typical five-day diet histories illustrate just how lacking the typical athlete's or consumer's diet can be in quality carbohydrates. These diet histories reflect three weekdays, plus Saturday and Sunday. Diet history 1 is for a fifteen-year-old female tennis player; diet history 2 is for a seventeen-year-old high school football player.

* * *

Diet History 1

	Breakfast	Lunch	Dinner	Snacks
Day 1	fried egg, white toast	chicken noodle soup, water, banana	pizza, Pepsi	
Day 2	pancakes, 2% milk	turkey sandwich on white bread, French roll, chips, water	chicken, rice, green salad, milk	chocolate ice cream
Day 3	toast, orange juice	pizza, green salad, chocolate cake	Chinese food, chocolate cake	nachos, cereal
Day 4	banana bread, milk	peanut butter and jelly sandwich on white bread, apple	hamburger, French fries, Coke	chips, bagel
Day 5	Cheerios cereal, milk	Snickers candy bar, apple	garlic chicken and rice, water	chips

* * *

Diet History 2

	Breakfast	**Lunch**	**Dinner**	**Snacks**
Day 1	3 doughnuts, milk	hamburger, French fries, Coke	spaghetti, green salad, garlic bread, milk	ice cream
Day 2	chocolate instant breakfast drink, 2 eggs, 2 pieces white toast	2 pieces of chicken, French fries, Coke, apple	lasagna with ricotta cheese, carrots, milk	cookies
Day 3	Cocoa Puffs cereal, milk, orange juice	bologna sandwich, lettuce, tomato, milk, chips, banana	BBQ beef, salad milk, rice	nachos, cereal
Day 4	Cocoa Puffs cereal, milk, orange juice, 2 pieces bacon	cheeseburger, French fries, Coke, Snickers candy bar	BBQ beef, salad, milk, baked potato	cookies
Day 5	pancakes, syrup, butter, milk, sausage	peanut butter and jelly sandwich, chips, Coke, grapes	pizza, Dr. Pepper	ice cream

The goal of these diet histories is not to obtain detailed portion sizes but trends in food choices, and these particular diet histories are typical for this age group. In diet history 1, the tennis player, only seven of the fifteen meals contained a fruit or a vegetable. What's more, this diet also shows very limited intake of quality grains or cereals. (Of course, this diet shows significant other nutritional problems, including a lack of calcium.) It is simply not possible for this athlete to recover the glycogen used in a strenuous Monday workout by Tuesday and maintain a high level of training throughout the week.

The subject of diet history 2, our high school football player, clearly is a bigger eater than the athlete in diet history 1. However, it wasn't until day 3 that this athlete consumed any significant quantities of fruit and vegetables with each meal, and on the other days he consumed two or three servings per day—insufficient for both his long-term health and for training purposes. Here again, quality grains, legumes, and cereals are consistently absent.

Both diets reflect a diet high in protein, fat, and refined carbohydrates but limited in quality carbohydrates, which is typical for most athletes. Given these two classic examples, why is it that many athletes and active consumers believe they need more protein in their diets, when the vast majority already consume more than enough? The answer is directly related to long-standing marketing hype from the supplement industry, aimed at an uneducated or misinformed audience. But you simply need to look at each meal and ask yourself these two questions:

Does this meal contain a fruit and/or vegetable and a quality grain, cereal, or legume?

Do most of my in-between meal snacks include more of the same?

By consistently answering yes to both questions, you will increase the percentage of quality carbohydrate content in your diet and reduce the fat and protein content to their appropriate percentages of 55 to 65 percent carbohydrates, 15 percent protein and 25 to 30 percent fat, with no more than one third of the fat intake coming from saturated fats. This will have an immediate impact on the your energy level and physical development capabilities, as well as on long-term health benefits, such as reduced rates of cancer, heart disease, diabetes, and obesity.

If the prognosis for those who've been ignoring the importance of carbohydrates sounds a little bleak, there's an upside. People who have been eating insufficient carbohydrates and who start eating sufficient quantities will quickly see major ergogenic and health benefits. I have observed athletes make significant gains in strength, endurance, and overall energy levels in as little as seven to ten days simply by including far more fruits, vegetables, breads, and cereals at each meal and for snacks. The sport supplement industry is well aware of this, as well, and some manufacturers have developed very simple yet effective deceptive marketing methods to take advantage of the fact that an increase in carb intake can quickly show dramatic results. They simply need to convince athletes that their product contains some "special" ingredient or combination of ingredients that will provide some or all of these basic carbohydrate benefits. That special ingredient can be ineffective or inert, as long as the supplement also contains the appropriate amount of carbohydrates that will bring about the desired results. The consumer who knows little about nutrition will assume the "special" ingredient did the trick.

Some might ask, what's wrong with that? If an athlete actually benefits from taking the supplement, why does it matter if he or she has been deceived? Most importantly, the taking of supplements can have a negative impact on one's health. No one supplement can provide all the plant chemicals found in food, and taking a supplement instead of consuming a well-balanced diet deprives the body of many of the compounds found in food. On top of this, simple carbohydrate supplements that claim to contain some "wonder" ingredient take advantage of consumers' ignorance or naiveté; the consumer would save money (and obtain the same results) simply by making better food choices. Nobody appreciates being swindled or considered a fool.

If carbohydrate-based supplements are a poor substitute for a healthy diet, protein products are even less reliable. When added to a diet that is providing insufficient calories for the energy demands, a powdered protein product will provide some much-needed extra calories and may indirectly improve performance and energy levels. However, these products provide benefits via a metabolic process that is very inefficient compared to what occurs when the body consumes carbohydrates from food. The simple problem of carbohydrate deficit is common knowledge to supplement companies, and they use it readily to perpetuate the myth that athletes need greater amounts of protein than their diets provide. And, as with carbohydrate supplements, most consumers will falsely associate improved levels of energy and training intensity with an ingredient in the supplement.

What is actually taking place is that the protein in the drink or powder is being converted—very inefficiently—into a carbohydrate. The liver must structurally change the protein into a glucose molecule and excrete the nitrogen attached to the original amino acid (protein molecule) before the body can use it as an energy source. This complex process is very inefficient compared to the body's direct metabolism of actual carbohydrates as an energy source. Additionally, the excess nitrogen, now no longer bound to the excess protein, must be diluted and then excreted. This can increase urine production two- to four-fold, which adds additional stress to maintaining adequate hydration levels.

Since limited muscle development is far more likely to be related to a carbohydrate deficit than to a protein deficit, an important question to consider is exactly how much carbohydrate we need in our diet. The standard answer from most professional sources is roughly 60 percent. But what do I do if my energy needs are still not being met? How do I know if my fatigue or apathy for training is carbohydrate related? The simplest method of matching carbohydrate intake to energy need is to consume an additional 200 calories per day strictly from carbohydrate foods for one to two weeks. The following list shows how easy it can be to add 200 calories from carb foods per day.

apple	1 medium	81 calories
banana	1 medium	105 calories
orange (navel)	1 medium	65 calories
pears, canned in light syrup	1 cup	144 calories
pineapple, canned in own juice	1 cup	150 calories
raisins	⅔ cup	302 calories
spaghetti	1 cup	216 calories
flour tortilla	1	95 calories
potato, white	1 medium	95 calories
corn, canned	⅗ cup	60 calories
corn on the cob	4-inch length	100 calories
peas	⅔ cup	71 calories
pancakes, plain homemade	1 medium	104 calories

Logic says that the addition of 200 calories per day will lead to an increase in body fat. However, there are three reasons why many athletes and active consumers do not gain fat from this approach. First, if you have been in a carbohydrate deficit, your muscle and liver will simply store the additional carbohydrate along with three times as much water as the carbohydrate weight. You'll see this additional sugar and water storage on the scale as increased body weight, but not fat weight. This is to your advantage.

Second, increasing carbohydrates may eliminate the early fatigue associated with carb deficit, allowing for an increase of training duration and intensity. In other words, you may have only been providing enough fuel for your muscles to work at a level considerably below what they are capable of. Now your body simply utilizes the extra calories. (This is why some athletes are able to increase their daily carbohydrate intake by as much as 500 calories with no fat weight gain.)

Third, the extra 200 calories from carbohydrate foods will more than likely replace some higher-fat food calories due to satiety, offsetting some, if not all, of the increased caloric intake.

If you increase your intake of quality carbohydrates at all meals and snacks, the protein intake from animal sources as well as fat intake, preferably from nuts, seeds, and whole grains, will take care of itself. In other words, dramatically increasing the percentage of quality carbohydrate intake naturally reduces the percentage of calories from protein and fat to a more appropriate level. Snacks should include breads, cereals, fruits, nuts, or seeds whenever possible. Eating nuts helps ensure that the diet includes enough fat from unsaturated sources. Remember that fatty acids, from stored body fat, can provide a significant portion of endurance athletes' energy demands.

Whether the fuel is stored sugar or fat, or a combination of the two, the extent to which the body utilizes it for energy depends on the following:

- Physical conditioning. An athlete's physical condition will dictate the muscles' ability to extract and utilize oxygen once it arrives. The level of conditioning is partly dependent upon the availability of sufficient carbohydrates.
- Dietary habits. If the diet is low in carbohydrates, the intensity and duration of the workout will diminish.

GREAT REASONS TO CONSUME MORE CARBOHYDRATES

- Carbohydrates are the primary fuel for the brain and the immune and nervous systems. Carbohydrate depletion affects not only the duration and intensity of physical exertion but also coordination, reaction time, and mental focus.

- When carbohydrates are deficient, the body will utilize protein for some of its energy needs. This prevents the use of protein for rebuilding injured tissue or building new tissue; it also increases your hydration needs due to the need to increase urine production and excrete any excess nitrogen from the once protein molecule.
- If carbohydrate intake is low, the intensity of activity must decrease in order to accommodate the increased burning of fatty acids, which are less efficiently oxidized at higher work rates than carbohydrates.
- High-intensity activities, such as sprinting, jumping, wrestling, etc., which require many short bursts of power, speed, or repetitive stop-and-go movements, rely almost entirely on stored glucose in the muscle tissue.

Hydration

Consider the following advertising claim for Product Y:

- Improved muscle function, strength, endurance, and development
- Improved heart function
- Improved waste product removal
- Improved concentration
- Faster recovery between workouts
- A decline of as little as 2 percent or 3 percent of this nutrient will *negatively* impact all the functions listed here.

How much would you pay for this wonder drug? Most of us can get it for free, or nearly so. How can it be, then, that while water has the most profound effect on our ability to physically train and perform, it is generally the second most ignored component of our day-to-day dietary habits?

Consider the following scenario describing a 180-pound male athlete. On Monday, this individual trains two hours and drops four pounds, or 2 percent of his body weight, due to the loss of body water. Between Monday's practice session and Tuesday's, he consumes only enough water to replace three of the four pounds he lost on Monday. On Tuesday he trains and loses four more pounds as a result of water loss and again replaces only three of the four pounds. By Wednesday this athlete begins practice with a body water deficit of two pounds, and by Thursday or Friday that deficit has increased to three or three and a half pounds, or roughly 2 percent of his body weight.

This common situation may result in significant losses in physical strength, endurance, reaction time, and coordination. It may also be accompanied by headache, apathy, and cramping. Considering the proven ability of a well-hydrated body to produce greater amounts of work for longer periods of time, it is amazing how many athletes and coaching personnel fail to monitor water intake.

To prevent not only the impaired exercise performance associated with a 2 percent to 3 percent loss of body fluids, but also its progression to potentially life-threatening heatstroke, follow these hydration guidelines, provided by the American College of Sports Medicine:

1. Stay well hydrated throughout the day. Most people tend to ignore the early signal from the thirst mechanism and wait until the motivation to drink is significant. A common misconception is that the thirst mechanism is inefficient. It actually is sufficient for most. Generally, the issue is if water is not immediately available, then the early stimulation to drink is ignored until there is enough actual physical discomfort associated with it that we finally stop what we are doing to seek fluid intake. If you feel a need to drink, then drink, do not wait.
2. Drink sixteen ounces of fluid one to three hours before exercise. This allows time for the fluid to be absorbed into the tissues and for any excess to be excreted prior to intense training or competition.

3. During exercise, attempt to drink six to twelve ounces of fluid at fifteen- to twenty-minute intervals beginning at the start of the workout.
4. Beverages containing carbohydrates in concentrations of 4 percent to 8 percent are recommended for intense exercise events lasting longer than one hour. For some athletes, the palatability of the sodium and sugar in a sports drink like Gatorade or Powerade encourages greater fluid intake.
5. Since most athletes do not consume enough fluids during exercise to balance fluid losses (including sweat and urine production), after exercise it might be necessary to consume up to 150 percent of the weight lost during the workout. More simply put, you need to consume roughly sixteen ounces of fluid for every pound lost during exercise, but to cover urine production and dehydrated cells and tissue, try to consume roughly twenty-four ounces of fluid for every pound lost.

In order to follow these guidelines effectively, you will need to weigh yourself before and after exercise. This is a typical recommendation, but it has a minor flaw for some athletes who fail to remember to remove sweat saturated clothing prior to the postexercise weigh-in. For example, my dry clothed weight before exercise may be 215, and my wet clothed weight after exercise may be 211 to 212. Using the American College of Sports Medicine guidelines, I should consume seventy-two to ninety-six ounces, or nine to twelve cups of water, after a heavy exercise session. But my clothes are now soaked with perspiration, and I need to calculate in that additional weight, which represents fluid loss. This may account for an additional one to two pounds of fluid loss, depending upon clothing, perspiration rate, body size, the length of time spent exercising, and other factors.

Simply weigh yourself before and after either naked or with just the basic undergarments.

The bottom line is that dehydration can happen easily and can be hard to remedy, unless you give hydration the appropriate attention throughout the day with consistent water intake. Individuals who are prone to cramps and who perspire very heavily might try a suggestion from Suzanne Nelson-Steen, D.Sc., R.D., of the University of Washington's Department of Intercollegiate Athletics. Dr. Steen states that athletes who have a history of cramping and produce sweat that taste salty should try adding "¼–½ teaspoon of salt to 16 ounces of Gatorade and . . . eat more salt in their daily diets." She also suggests that cramp-prone athletes salt their food and "drink 20 ounces of salted Gatorade before games and practices" (*GSSI Conditioning and Nutrition for Football* Rt. #44 Vol. 12 (2001)—Number 2). This can be done with Powerade as well.

Since muscle mass is predominately water, any significant dehydration of this tissue will not only affect performance but will also diminish the ability to burn or utilize excess body fat or maintain a desired weight. Water is essential for dissipating the heat produced by muscle tissue during exercise (fifteen to twenty times the heat produced at resting levels); without a steady water supply, this heat can potentially increase the core body temperature to a life-threatening level. To prevent this, when muscle tissues heat up the brain simply curtails the central nervous system stimulus of the tissue in order to prevent any further rise in body temperature. This results in lethargy or fatigue unrelated to the lack of the necessary fuel source and diminishes performance, intensity levels, and the body's ability to burn excess body fat.

Water's thermoregulatory effects are so critical that all athletes and active consumers should be aware of the symptoms of dehydration. However, there is no need to overhydrate, and it is a myth that all individuals need a specific amount of water per day. A body's water requirements vary dramatically depending upon activity level, body size, ambient conditions, types of food consumed, and perspiration rates. For most people, the combination of being sensitive and responsive to the thirst mechanism along with monitoring weight loss from activity is sufficient to maintain good hydration.

Overzealous efforts of hydration, often indicated by frequently voiding significant amounts of clear urine, can lead to a condition called hyponatremia. Sometimes observed in endurance athletes, this condition involves such an excess ingestion of hypotonic fluids (water with limited or no sodium content) that the body's normal concentration of this mineral becomes overly diluted. Symptoms associated with hyponatremia are malaise, confusion, nausea, and fatigue in moderate cases and coma, seizures, and possibly death in more severe cases.

SYMPTOMS OF DEHYDRATION

2 percent water loss	Vague discomfort, fatigue, headache, and apathy
3 percent water loss	Decrease in muscular endurance
5 percent water loss	The above plus muscle cramps, decreased muscle strength, and, if left untreated, heat exhaustion.
Heat exhaustion	The above plus rapid pulse, fever, central nervous system dysfunction, and confusion
7 percent water loss or greater	The above plus hallucinations, circulatory collapse, and possible death

Along with the watching for the symptoms, athletes should keep in mind the following potential causes of dehydration:

1. Protein supplements or high-protein diets can increase urine output two- to fourfold as the body attempts to eliminate the excess nitrogen that results from excess protein intake.
2. Alcoholic beverages increase urine output. Never consume alcohol before or after training or competing.

3. High humidity inhibits or prevents sweat from evaporating. This inhibits the release of heat generated by working muscles, resulting in a rapid rise in body core temperature to potentially dangerous levels.
4. Wearing too much clothing, sauna suits, or other excess gear can hinder or prevent the normal dissipation of heat. People sometimes wear these items with the mistaken idea that they will assist in the reduction of body fat. Remember that body fat is roughly 5 percent to 20 percent water by weight. The fluids lost from perspiration come from the blood volume and muscle tissue, *not* from body fat. What's more, the excess water loss will only hinder fat loss due to the obstruction of muscle function. Once the muscles become dehydrated, their ability to perform work is significantly diminished.
5. Caffeine is often reported as a diuretic. However, an excellent review published by the American College of Sports Medicine, Caffeine and Exercise Performance, states, "The available literature does not support immediate diuretic effect as body core temperature, sweat loss, plasma volume and urine volume were unchanged during exercise following caffeine ingestion."

7 BODY COMPOSITION AND WEIGHT CONTROL

A REALITY CHECK

Over half the population in both the United States and Europe is overweight (some estimates are as high as two-thirds), due in large part to our predominantly sedentary lifestyles and poor dietary habits. The causes of much of this obesity begin in childhood and include inactivity, poor food choices, and frequent overeating. By the time many individuals are mature enough to understand the negative effects of this behavior on their health and physical abilities, it's often too late for anything more than modest changes.

Less than a century ago, dietary fat played an essential role in allowing individuals to maintain the intensity of labor that daily life required. This is no longer the case in the United States and other industrialized countries, where we see increasing rates of obesity in both children and adults. In short, we are a society of the under-exercised and overfed.

The combination of limited physical activity and excessive food intake has serious health consequences, predisposing millions to premature heart disease, early mortality, arthritis, diabetes, hernias, respiratory problems, and possibly several forms of cancer. Many overweight people develop a general disinterest in physical exercise, often because of the discomfort associated with moving a large body of mass that may have overstressed or arthritic joints.

While losing body fat has dozens of health benefits, many people are motivated to do so by other factors, such as appearance, improved athletic performance, or work productivity. This longing to lose body fat has spawned an industry that preys upon millions of consumers. In desperation, many people succumb to a "what if" mentality: Sure, this product's claims are probably false, but "What if it works?"

Meanwhile, there is no end to the misinformation about weight control, and no shortage of snake oil salesmen willing to accommodate us with their potions, nostrums, and programs. When it comes to our physical appearance and our health, even otherwise sensible people can find themselves taken in by deceptive claims. But consumers who arm themselves with a basic understanding of body composition and its functions will have reasonable expectations about losing body fat and will protect themselves from the supplement industry's clever and deceptive claims.

Body Fat Basics

The average eighteen- to thirty-year-old athletic adult of normal weight has roughly 25 to 30 billion fat cells. The average man has roughly 9,000 grams (81,000 calories) of fat storage. These billions of fat cells are necessary for survival in many undeveloped regions of the world, but not in industrialized countries like the United States. Here, poor lifestyle choices often cause these 30 billion cells to expand and expand, both in size and number. The total number of fat cells in an obese individual can be approximately three times more than in a healthy weight person (on average, 75 billion compared to 27 billion); very obese adults can have as many as 260 billion fat cells! Even more significant, in an obese person the fat content of each cell is roughly 35 percent greater than that in a person of healthy weight (Lea & Febigers, *Exercise Physiology, Energy, Nutrition, and Human Performance*, 2nd edition, pg. 535.)

Although it is possible to dramatically change the size or content of these fat cells by losing body fat, the *number* of cells and their ability to quickly regain weight remain the same. For example, an overweight adult weighing 328 pounds has roughly 75 billion fat cells; if his weight dropped to 165 pounds, he would still have 75 billion fat cells.

This truth about fat cells is a major reason why so many individuals regain any weight they've lost. There simply is no question that formerly obese individuals will always find it very difficult to maintain a healthier weight. The only road to long-term weight loss success is permanent adherence to the appropriate lifestyle changes.

Fat cells have relatively little water content (15–20 percent at most) and are not nearly as dense or heavy as water molecules. (This is why overweight individuals find it easier to float than do leaner or more muscular individuals.) Other body fuels require more water content in order to be metabolized; for example, every gram of stored sugar in muscle and the liver must retain 2.7 grams of water, roughly a 3-to-1 ratio. If our bodies were designed to carry all our stored energy needs as sugar, the water that the body would have to retain to metabolize that sugar would add considerable weight to our frames (approximately fifty pounds!) and would greatly inhibit muscular movement.

With their low water content, it's obvious we can't "sweat off" body fat cells. Trying to reduce the size of a fat cell by sweating off its already limited water content will lead only to dehydration of the muscle mass and cardiovascular system—which actually *impedes* body fat loss. Once you become dehydrated by as little as 3 percent of your total body weight, the efficient functioning of both the muscles and the cardiovascular systems is greatly reduced. That results in a significant decline in the amount of body fat that can be delivered to the muscle tissue for oxidation and the production of energy or work.

The most productive way to reduce body fat over time, and to keep it off long term, is to increase training or exercise time while at the same time reducing daily caloric intake by 300 to 500 calories. Athletes should make these adjustments several months prior to the competitive season to avoid the lethargy that can accompany weight loss efforts and hinder training intensity. (Keep in mind, too, that rapid weight loss can precipitate a loss of muscle mass, strength, and power; mental exhaustion; depressed immunity; and mood changes.) Active adults without the concerns of athletic competition can begin efforts to lose excess body fat at any time. For adults who have never participated in a rapid weight loss program, the combination of increased exercise and decreased food should allow a loss of one to two pounds of body fat—not weight—per week.

If you've participated in a weight loss program for a month or longer in which the total daily caloric intake was 500 to 800 calories, your body may have become very efficient in the absorption and retention of calories. In response to these very-low-calorie diets, the body adapts by lowering the basal metabolic rate (the number of calories the body utilizes at rest). The body can also respond to low calorie intake by increasing the efficiency of its absorption and retention in fat cells, an adaptation that significantly hinders long-term efforts to maintain a desirable weight or lose future unwanted body fat.

Weight loss from caloric restriction alone, of more than two pounds per week is simply an unrealistic goal, and the methods for achieving that kind of weight loss can have serious negative training effects. The sharp reduction in calories (and the corresponding reduction of carbohydrate and fat in the diet) required to do this can significantly impact training intensity, duration, possibly testosterone levels, decreased immunity, decreased concentration, and chronic fatigue.

Trying to lose more than one to two pounds of body fat per week through increased exercise alone has its risks as well; for both active adults and well-conditioned athletes, any large increases in training time or intensity can precipitate structural damage to bones, tendons, ligaments, or muscles that were unprepared to tolerate a sudden increase in activity.

Physical therapists often see the results of this kind of dietary and exercise manipulation. Well-intentioned couch potatoes or moderately active adults suddenly become motivated to make changes, but their conception of what is possible is not in line with what their bodies are capable of doing. Instead of taking a safe and conservative approach, they try to undo in one month what has taken a couple of years to accomplish with limited activity and poor dietary habits.

Athletes can also be prone to self-deception, becoming overconfident about their physical abilities. While they may be tough enough mentally for the challenge, they soon realize that they have pushed their bodies beyond what they are capable of tolerating. This lesson comes far too frequently as we get older. It is a piece of wisdom that's difficult to pass along to those in their teens or twenties who still believe they're invincible—that view that always changes with time.

Basal Metabolic Rate

The basal metabolic rate is the body's total caloric requirement over a twenty-four-hour period to sustain all its functions at rest, including vital organ functions, maintaining body temperature, thought processes, and respiration. Average basal rates are 1,100 to 1,450 calories per day for females and 1,500 to 1,800 calories per day for males, depending on body size, age, muscle mass, climate (basal metabolic rates are lower in warm climates), state of nutrition, presence of disease, and other factors. Larger athletic females and males would have BMRs considerably higher. You can positively change your BMR by becoming more physically active and increasing the amount of muscle mass. You can negatively effect your BMR (reduce it) by becoming sedentary, losing muscle mass, or excessive caloric restriction such as the once popular 800 calorie diets. Aging naturally reduces the BMR due to declining physical activity, muscle mass, and testosterone levels.

I once ran an exercise physiology lab for a large medical practice, where we tested patients' cardiopulmonary (heart and lung) and cardiovascular functions. At the request of an endocrinologist, I often measured the resting basal rate for obese patients who were suspected to have underactive thyroids. I took the measurement after a twenty-four-hour period of no physical activity, and a twelve-hour fast.

On one occasion I had two who were patients who were about to begin a very restricted caloric intake (800 calories per day) at another medical facility. Prior to this caloric restriction, their BMRs were 1,100–1,200. After they had been on the low-calorie diets for three to four weeks, both patients had lowered their basal metabolic rates by 200 calories per day. This is a natural protective mechanism by the brain to prevent what it interprets as insufficient calories to maintain vital organ function and all the related physiological functions that take place twenty-four hours per day seven days a week. Theoretically, this loss in resting caloric expenditure would be equivalent to burning off twenty pounds of body fat over the year.

The basal rate adaptation I observed is consistent with medical literature on the subject, which demonstrates that such a reduction in BMR can be permanent if rapid weight loss dieting is repeated. This is one reason why many individuals who choose rapid weight loss programs find themselves regaining the weight very quickly after resuming normal eating patterns. Their bodies simply have become far more efficient at gaining weight from any excess caloric intake.

Sadly, some individuals who have engaged in repeated bouts of crash dieting may experience weight gain from consuming any more than 800 to 900 calories per day (*Total Nutrition: The Only Guide You Will Ever Need*, Mount Sinai School of Medicine 1995, pg. 297). Moreover, rapid weight loss can result in reduced muscle mass, which further hinders long-term efforts to utilize excess body fat. Extended periods of caloric deficit precipitate the breaking down of muscle for use as calories and other components that are not being provided by the diet. Simply put, faced with an extreme shortage of calories, your body begins to eat itself (anorexia).

The Genetic Link

Many individuals are genetically predisposed to obesity; their bodies may store fat more efficiently, reconvert stored fat back to available energy less efficiently, use their calories more efficiently, or produce excess amounts of the enzyme lipoprotein lipase, which allows fat and muscle cells to absorb fatty acids. The number of individuals this predisposition effects is unknown, and the exact mechanisms behind it are not yet completely understood. Since we are all part of the same basic genetic pool (the human genome is 99.9% the same in all people), this predisposition exists among people all over the world, but we see more obesity in the United States and other industrialized countries due to diminished physical demands, greater availability of food, and excessive intake of high caloric foods.

However, even individuals predisposed to obesity have a personal responsibility to take care of their health by making good lifestyle choices. Just like someone whose genetic makeup includes diabetes, these individuals must closely monitor daily food and exercise requirements to maintain good health. Moreover, tossing in the towel on weight control will only worsen a genetic predisposition to excessive fat weight gain. It can even play a role in your becoming physically dependent upon others later in life.

Aside from obesity's personal toll, consider the enormous medical costs society must bear for the treatment of illnesses associated with obesity, including diabetes, arthritis, joint replacement surgeries, heart disease, and some forms of cancer. As we get heavier and heavier as a nation, this escalating financial burden is passed along to each succeeding generation. My children and your children will help pay for the cost of medical complications associated with obesity.

Bear in mind, though, that this genetic predisposition for excess weight is only one of several risk factors for obesity; genetics alone will not make an individual obese. Several other factors, including behavior and environmental conditions, combine with heredity to cause obesity.

Consider the Pima Indians of Arizona, reportedly one of the heaviest groups of people in the world. The Pima Indians who live in remote areas of Mexico in a physically demanding environment, on the other hand, are reportedly as lean as other non-Pima Mexicans living in the same region (*American Journal of Clinical Nutrition*, 1998; 68: 1,053–7). Assuming the inheritable gene pool is similar for both groups of Pima Indians, a likely explanation for the excess weight of those in Arizona is that they have access to more food or they do less physical activity or the combination of both.

Recent research published in the *Annals of Internal Medicine* (1999; 130: 873–82) supports this finding. In this study, researchers compared the behavioral habits and body fat of 485 sets of female twins. They found that regular physical activity was the strongest independent predictor of total-body fat. The sisters who had higher levels of physical activity than their siblings also had nearly nine pounds average less body fat. Even with a genetic predisposition to excessive weight gain, regular exercise is associated with significantly lower levels of body fat and greater physical independence and better health as we age.

Whether or not an overweight person is genetically predisposed to obesity, chances are the problem with excess weight began in childhood. Without good guidance from parents, too many children grow up in households where they are allowed to be sedentary, where they never develop an appreciation for running and playing outside for hours at a time, and where they overindulge in poor food choices. But there are a number of significant variables that contribute to a particular individual's body size, and stereotyping overweight individuals as lazy or undisciplined amounts to simple ignorance, and arrogance.

> ***Females and Weight Control***
>
> Let us not forget that weight control problems also arise at the other end of the eating spectrum. Due to the national obsession with body fat, fourth- and fifth-grade girls of perfectly healthy weight are openly concerned about "being fat." Many, even those of normal weight, are dieting. A study published in 1988 (*American Journal of Diseases in Children,* 1988; 142: 1114–18) showed that 54 percent of 854 adolescent girls and young women surveyed were dissatisfied with their current body shape, and 67 percent were dissatisfied with their weight. In another study of 1,900 adolescents age twelve to sixteen, the authors reported that 52 percent of the normal weight Caucasian girls interviewed considered themselves overweight. The found that Caucasian girls were more than twice as likely to diet as African American girls, and six times more likely than Caucasian boys. The authors reported, "Adolescents' perception of their body weight is dependent on social, cultural, and family pressures" (*Archives of Pediatric and Adolescent Medicine,* 1999; 153; 741–47).

The preoccupation with body fat is a result of negative cultural influences, shaped in large part by the fashion industry through magazines and other media. Peer pressure is another factor; there are significant social stigmas and psychological impacts connected with body fat. All these forces fuel the $20- to $30-billion-a-year weight loss industry, which promotes largely ineffective long-term body fat reduction programs that have a high failure rate after one year. The sheer number of products marketed to address the issue of body weight reflects the anguish millions of females feel about their current weight.

The combination of social pressures and the need to have some control over their lives leads many young women to bulimia, anorexia, and other behavioral habits that are counterproductive to good health and athletic training. A study in the *Postgraduate Medical Journal* (1998, Vol. 74, pp. 473–79) noted that a growing number of teenage girls start or continue smoking because they believe it prevents weight gain. Based on a study of 2,800 British and Canadian schoolgirls ages ten to seventeen, researchers made the striking finding that many girls are willing to risk all the negative health consequences of smoking for less body fat (ironic, considering the long-term negative physical appearance of "smoker wrinkles" and stained teeth, not to mention heart disease and lung cancer).

The tendency among American female athletes and active adults to overstate their perceived "weight problem" leads many—even those of perfectly healthy weight—to reduce their caloric intake so much that it can't sustain intense training. Often this distorted perception of the body also prevents girls and women from increasing their caloric intake to accommodate increased training and other physical needs. In either case, not eating well leads to increased injuries and limited performance and strength gains.

This inadequate caloric intake can result in "false anorexia." (In false anorexia, the body weight and musculoskeletal development continue to appear reasonably normal for the girl's height and age, whereas true anorexics usually appear emaciated. True anorexics have an array of psychological fears related to food and body fat, which are not shared by most false anorexics.)

False anorexia, which leads to bone demineralization and amenorrhea (cessation of the menstrual cycle), occurs when the hypothalamus perceives caloric needs to be 2,500 to 3,000 calories per day to sustain vital organ function, energy needs, and growth, but the diet provides only 1,200 to 1,800 calories. Perceiving the body as starving, the hypothalamus imposes adaptations to protect the vital organs and prevent pregnancy, lowering the basal metabolic rate by 200 to 300 calories per day to conserve body fat, and perhaps stopping the production of estrogen, which results in the discontinuation of the menstrual cycle. Estrogen is necessary for the depositing of calcium into the bones; therefore, no estrogen production means that bone mass deposition is greatly inhibited. The combination of diminished bone development and calcium withdrawal from bones is likely to produce a bone demineralization process that can leave some twenty- to twenty-five-year-old women with bone mass similar to a fifty-year-old's. Bone mass development is critical between ages fifteen and twenty-five in order to prevent potentially debilitating osteoporosis later in life. Any time menstruation ceases, the cause should be determined and treated as soon as possible, especially in very young women.

Young females should pay particular attention to good dietary habits and get reasonable amounts of physical activity to ensure that strong, thick bones are in place by the time they reach menopause. Because of unnecessary dietary fat phobia, many young women unnecessarily forego high-calcium food sources like cheese, milk, cottage cheese, and yogurt. All these foods have a place in the daily diet and can make a dramatic difference in the prevention of osteoporosis.

Males and Weight Control

Males often find it easier than females to reduce excess body fat. For a man with well-conditioned muscles, his relatively larger heart allows a greater volume of blood and free fatty acids to be delivered to the muscle per minute. Similarly, a generally larger lung capacity allows greater quantities of oxygen to be sent to the muscle mass.

Males also can develop greater amounts of muscle mass due to significantly greater amounts of the hormone testosterone. This larger overall volume of muscle mass permits increased fatty acid oxidation during exercise and a higher basal metabolic rate while at rest.

Unfortunately, males are just as likely as females to have poor dietary habits and to hold misconceptions about body composition and weight control. A lack of good science education leads to far too much reliance on anecdotal misinformation from peers, bodybuilding or "health"-related magazines, and other media sources.

Weight Loss Myths and Misconceptions

Even if you're ready to commit to the diet and exercise necessary for losing or maintaining weight, common myths and misconceptions can sabotage your efforts. Some of the following are perpetrated by the dietary supplement and weight loss industries, and others are simple misunderstandings about how the body works.

"THE IDEAL BODY WEIGHT."

There simply is no such thing as an ideal body weight. There are desirable or healthy weight ranges for any body type, but these are interwoven with how the individual functions physically and feels emotionally at a particular weight. For instance, when body fat levels are too low, many athletes or active adults experience increased rates of illness, diminished performance, and chronic lethargy. These can be indicators that you have gone too far in fat reduction.

"MODERATE-CALORIE DIETS DO NOT WORK."

This misconception is often repeated in both professional journals and publications for general readers. We often hear that 90 to 95 percent of all overweight individuals who lose weight will regain what they lost, and often gain more. However, this data reflected only the failure rate of a relatively small number of subjects who have participated in various university based research programs. While it is true that the percentage of Americans who are obese is increasing, this percentage is far more reflective of long-standing poor lifestyle habits than it is of the physical inability to lose weight or to prevent excessive weight gain through a commitment to better lifestyle choices.

The good news is that when people make appropriate lifestyle changes and achieve gradual fat loss over a long period of time (eight months to a year), long-term positive changes can and do occur.

"LOW-FAT OR NONFAT FOODS WILL NOT MAKE YOU FAT."

Recently I was surprised to read in a professional nutrition journal the statement that you cannot gain excessive body fat from eating too many carbohydrates! The author has good credentials and works at a well-respected university—but he is dead wrong. It is true that your body will utilize significantly more excess calories from carbohydrates (roughly 20 to 25 percent) than from dietary fat (roughly 3 to 5 percent) to convert them to body fat. Possibly the author was referring to complex carbohydrates and was suggesting that most individuals consuming them would reach satiety quickly because of their high fiber content. Most people will certainly be unwilling to consume excessive quantities of complex carbohydrates in the form of high-fiber vegetables and whole grains. But you most certainly can develop and/or enlarge body fat cells by consuming excess quantities of *any* source of calories.

"MY METABOLISM IS TOO LOW."

An individual's resting metabolism rate is reflective of a number of factors, including body size, age, gender, genetics, lean muscle mass, and possibly physical condition. Unless they have a diagnosed hypothyroid problem, most people's resting energy expenditure will fall into normal ranges.

Many people find that they put on body fat more easily as they age. This is attributable both to lifestyle choices and to the decline in muscle mass associated with aging. Most adults simply experience dramatic reductions in physical activity as they age, while continuing to consume the same number of calories.

"SYNEPHRINE (BITTER ORANGE)-BASED PRODUCTS HAVE BEEN PROVEN TO BE SAFE AND EFFECTIVE."

A number of synephrine-containing products are being marketed as aids to weight loss. Synephrine stimulates the central nervous system, and its side effects can include significant increases in heart rates and blood pressure, and increased energy. This stimulation of the central nervous system leads many to believe that synephrine use directly correlates to increased body fat utilization, but this is not supported by current, well-designed studies. Synephrine, as ephedrine was, is combined with caffeine to increase its stimulatory effects—and of course the side effects increase as well.

If synephrine provides the "impulse" for users to become more physically active, then obviously it can play an indirect role in weight loss and/or maintenance. But any positive results that might be obtained by using this "motivating factor" must be weighed against potential serious health risks. When you consider that any possible long-term results that can be obtained by using synephrine-based products can also be obtained without its use, combined with its potential for severe health consequences, the obvious question is: Why do it?

"I'LL BURN MORE FAT IF I EXERCISE AT A LOWER INTENSITY."

This is not so much a myth as a misunderstanding of physiological processes. I hear this line routinely from patients who've picked the notion up at the gym, from a personal trainer, or from a training partner. It's true that at lower levels of intensities, you burn *proportionally* more fat. But the key word here is *proportional*, not *total*. Consider this example: If you walk 3 miles in one hour and burn 300 total calories, and 70 percent of those calories came from fat, you've burned 210 fat calories. If you jog for one hour and burn roughly 800 calories, only 50 percent of the required fuel will be derived from fat (400 fat calories), due to the higher intensity of jogging and the greater dependency on stored sugar. Nevertheless, you've burned almost *double* the total fat calories that you burned at a lower intensity level—which clearly will have a greater impact on reducing or maintaining a desired body fat level. Not everyone wants to or can jog for an hour. The point is that whatever form of exercise you choose, as long as it's aerobic in nature and you can do it for thirty minutes or more at a time, the total amount of fat you will burn will be greater at higher intensities than lower ones.

"I'M SO EXHAUSTED FROM WORKING OUT— I MUST HAVE BURNED A LOT OF FAT."

Unfortunately, it is a false assumption that an exhausting physical effort equals a significant use of calories or body fat. By design, our muscle tissue is capable of generating a large number of contractions with relatively little energy expenditure. (If this mechanism were less effective, millions of people around the world who have relatively little to eat would be unable to sustain the level of physical labor needed to survive.) Put simply, your engine is very fuel-efficient. Moreover, there is wide variation in the human capacity to run these fuel-efficient engines hard enough and long enough to burn stored fuel.

One pound of fat in the body holds 3,500 calories. A well-conditioned endurance athlete who has undergone intense training may be capable of expending 800 to 1,200 calories for one hour of endurance activity (not including the necessary extended cool-down period). But even if that athlete burns the maximum, 1,200 calories in an hour, it's clear that he simply could not lose one pound of fat in one day, unless he ate little or nothing all day. (Making that level of fat loss even more unobtainable, a significant portion of the energy the athlete is using is coming from stored sugar, not from fat.)

Looking at it another way, to burn all the energy provided by one pound of fat, you'd have to walk 35 miles (100 calories/mile)—and again, you'd have to be relying totally on fat for your energy source, which is not how the body functions. The simple truth is that it is physiologically impossible for anyone to lose one pound of body fat a day under normal circumstances. Any diet or exercise program that produces weight loss (not fat loss) of one pound a day or more is relying on a loss of water weight, which occurs when the body sweats to cool down working muscles. That quick drop in "weight" on the scale has little to do with a reduction of stored body fat.

You can see why patience is so important to any weight loss effort. Most athletes and other healthy, well-conditioned adults will probably require a minimum of three months of consistent effort to lose twelve to twenty-four pounds of fat. (The exact amount of fat lost will depend not only on physical activity and dietary habits but also on body size, age, gender, and current level of physical conditioning.)

"ALL YOU HAVE TO DO IS GET THE FAT OUT OF THE DIET."

Dietary fat is not the demon many would have you believe. Dietary fat plays an important role in maintaining health, including assisting in the transport of the fat-soluble vitamins A, D, E, and K across the intestines, and supplying the essential fatty acid linoleic acid, which is involved in many biological functions, including growth, cell membranes structure, and the production of prostaglandins.

Research has also shown that fat stored within the muscle fiber (not the fat under your skin) plays an important role in metabolism at exercise intensities as high as 80 percent of maximal effort. The fatigue an endurance athlete feels is often associated with depletion of either glycogen or fat stored within the fibers themselves. This readily available fat depot can account for about 3,000 calories verses the 1,200 or so stored as glycogen.

With the current negative views of fat, far too many overzealous athletes and active adults attempt to unnecessarily exclude fat from their diets. More sensibly, we simply need to determine what amount of fat is appropriate for our genetic makeup and lifestyle. For example, an endurance athlete whose training requires him to consume roughly 4,000 to 5,000 calories per day might need to have as much as 40 percent of his calories to come from fat to provide enough energy to maintain quality training sessions. The increased fat intake should come from monounsaturated fatty foods, like almonds, peanuts, peanut butter, walnuts, cashews, olives, and olive oil. At the other end of the spectrum is a minimally active, overweight adult with a sedentary job who has high cholesterol and a family history of premature heart disease. This individual, like most moderately active adults, might need to maintain a fat intake no higher than 20 to 25 percent of total calories to achieve and maintain a healthier physical profile.

Once you determine your individual needs, the necessary dietary and lifestyle changes for losing or maintaining weight should be fairly easy to identify. Of course, you'll also have to apply will and discipline, as well as knowledge, to achieve your goal.

Some Tips for Sensible Weight Control

The bottom line: the most effective and lasting way to reduce body fat is to increase physical activity and decrease calories. It's essential, too, to maintain healthy eating habits. Here are some simple rules of thumb that will help eliminate the 300 to 500 calories per day necessary to shed body fat:

- Eat at home as often as possible. This will help you avoid the high-fat and calorie-rich foods on restaurant menus. It takes a lot of discipline to turn down a tasty BLT and a chocolate shake.
- If you have to eat meals away from home, bring your own healthful option whenever you can.

- Do not keep addictive snack foods (chips, candy, ice cream, etc.) in the house unless you are capable of keeping portion sizes reasonable. Pick two or three nights a week to have one of these with a meal or as dessert.
- Try to prevent late-night grazing. Brush and floss your teeth soon after dinner. The hassle of rebrushing can be enough to prevent the 10 p.m. refrigerator raid.
- Try to be active every day. The activity doesn't have to be intense; expending even an extra 100 calories a day on fun physical activities will account for 10 pounds a year (100 calories x 365 days = 36,500/3,500 calories = 10.4 pounds). Simply turn off the TV and find something more constructive to do with your time, like walking a mile while you visit with family or friends.

Of course, weight loss is not the only benefit to be gained through these efforts. Far too many people measure the success of a diet and fitness routine by their body weight, and not by their improved physical function. But even those whose weight or physical condition is very limiting can make positive changes in their lives by adhering to a daily exercise program and better food choices. These improvements in quality of life can include:

- improved balance,
- improved blood sugar levels in diabetics,
- improved blood pressure,
- increased strength,
- better sleep,
- improved stamina,
- greater productivity at work,
- climbing stairs unassisted, and
- physical independence as you age.

We all have our limitations; it will take some of us a little longer to get to the top of the hill, but we do eventually arrive, and we will have enjoyed the same scenery even if we've had to stop occasionally and take in a much longer view of our surroundings before proceeding. To knowingly increase our limitations—genetic or otherwise—through further neglect of physical condition and diet is not only irresponsible, it also greatly limits our ability to enjoy what life has to offer.

Sensible weight loss or weight control is achieved only with good choices—choices about not only food and exercise but about diets and diet aids. At the same time that you're committing to physical activity and better eating habits, be sure to avoid the following:

- High-protein or high-fat diets. These regimens deplete stored sugars in the muscle and liver. What's more, the dehydration that often accompanies such a dietary plan inhibits the ability of muscle tissues to dissipate heat generated during exercise; in order to prevent overheating, the body diminishes muscle activity, which causes lethargy and prevents the optimal utilization of body fat. (In these diets, the added high-protein or high-fat foods also tend to take the place of healthful carbohydrates.)
- Diets that eliminate or limit complex carbohydrates. Along with eliminating thousands of plant chemicals found in carbohydrate foods that are essential for good health, a diet low in carbohydrates causes a significant drop in stored glycogen (energy) in muscle and liver tissue, which leads to lethargy, an inability to sustain intensity levels or duration, decreased co-ordination and reaction time, lack of concentration and reaction time, and possibly reduced testosterone levels. Consuming carbohydrates also causes a rise in the body's production of insulin, a hormone that "unlocks" the cells and

allows fuel (carbohydrate) and protein to enter. Without this response, the muscle tissue would fail to adapt to training by rebuilding and repairing itself and would decrease its capacity to burn body fat for energy. Studies have shown that there is no difference in weight loss after one year on a low-carbohydrate diet compared to a diet reduced in total calories, especially fat (*Annals of Internal Medicine,* May 18, 2004).

- Diets that fall below 2,000 to 2,500 calories for females in training or 3,000 to 3,500 calories for males in training. Recall that the average BMR alone will range from 1,100 to 1,400 for females and as high as 1,800 for males. Also remember that a well-trained athlete could utilize 800–1,200 calories/hour during training sessions. So consuming too few calories will inhibit training intensity and duration as the week progresses because there would not be sufficient calories from carbohydrates to replenish the stored sugar (glycogen). This would actually inhibit fat loss in the long-term.
- Fasting, unless for religious purposes. Fasting would obviously eliminate any restoration of stored muscle or liver sugar used during training or competing.
- Meal replacement wannabes. These typically are unbalanced and costly and have no long-term benefit. The so-called "meal replacement" items are especially misleading. For example, a meal replacement product might include beta-carotene on its ingredient label, but food includes hundreds of other important carotenoids that the product does not contain. These products cannot take the place of food, and claims that they do are simply deceptive hype. You can make your own for the fraction of the cost by trying the following recipe taken from the text *Nutrition Concepts and Controversies,* Tenth Edition pg. 383: Try 8 oz fat-free milk, 4 oz ice milk, 3 heaping tsp malted milk powder. For even higher carbohydrate and calorie val-

ues, blend in one-half banana or one-half cup of fruit. According to the text, compared to the average cost of three commercial formulas of about $2 per serving, the homemade version will cost about 50 cents per serving.

- Diet pills. The side effects from ingredients in these pills, such as phenylpropanolamine (PPA), can include headaches, blurred vision, rapid pulse, excessive sweating, heart palpitations, and increased blood pressure. And in the long run these pills simply are ineffective.
- Any synephrine or bitter orange-based products. According to the Natural Medicines Comprehensive Database, synephrine (bitter orange) "seems to cause many of the same side effects as ephedra. Bitter orange has been linked with ischemia stroke, myocardial infarction, arrhythmia, and syncope."
- Sauna suits. Body fat contains relatively little water, so the fluids lost with the use of sauna suits come from muscle and blood volume. The resulting dehydration will only hinder fat loss efforts by reducing the optimal functioning of your cardiovascular and musculoskeletal systems, which in turns reduces the overall oxidation of body fat. Staying well hydrated is essential for optimal body fat loss.
- Creams advertised to remove "cellulite" (just another marketing name for "fat"). Cellulite is the dimpled fat on the buttocks or thighs of women. This fat tissue is no different than fat tissue found elsewhere on the body. The dimpling or bulging appearance of this fat tissue is attributed to the bands of fibrous tissue located in this area.
- Anything promoted with terms like *miraculous*, *fast*, *easy*, *effortless*, *while you sleep*, and so on. Most people will agree that it certainly is "miraculous, fast, easy, effortless, it happened while I slept, etc." to put on excess body fat, but the opposite is not true, and it never will be. It is far easier to prevent

> excessive accumulation of body fat than it is to take it off. If most weight loss programs were even remotely successful, the current national problem with obesity would be minimal.

One last important point is that individuals who are considering a commercially available weight control program should bear in mind the significant amount of false and deceptive advertising associated with the weight loss industry. Since 1988 the Federal Trade Commission has filed formal complaints against seventy-six companies for "unsubstantiated weight loss and weight-loss maintenance claims, atypical consumer testimonials and misleading staff credentials and endorsements" (www.ftc.gov.). The companies involved in these settlements are listed on the FTC Web site, but the fact that any company is *not* listed there should not be seen as an endorsement. The FTC cannot take action against each and every falsely advertised nostrum or program in the marketplace. It is up to consumers to use common sense and educate themselves fully before purchasing any product.

8 PRACTICAL APPLICATIONS

PUTTING IT ALL TOGETHER

The concept couldn't be simpler: Good nutrition plays a vital role in both short- and long-term health. Nevertheless, myths, misconceptions, and false advertising have turned the relatively straightforward process of nutrition into a complex quagmire of dos and don'ts.

How can people without a degree in nutrition navigate the hype? Let's begin by reviewing eight important points.

- The supplement industry's deceptive marketing methods have been well documented. You should not consider supplement manufacturers to be reliable sources of objective information about diet and nutrition. To protect both your health and your pocketbook, become familiar with these marketing techniques, and avoid any product that uses them.
- Three natural mechanisms allow all healthy individuals to maintain nutrient balance (homeostasis), for a wide range of diets, without any dietary supplements. This is true regardless of activity level, with the possible exception of premenopausal

females, some of whom may require iron supplements, possibly folate for sexually active females, and calcium for females who are at risk for the development of osteoporosis. Furthermore, it is a misapplication of recommended daily allowances (RDAs) to suggest that an individual must ingest 100 percent of the RDA every day to maintain the maximum benefit of any nutrient. The body's storage capacity for all nutrients is much greater than most people realize. Moreover, the body has the ability to increase nutrient absorption rates and recycling or retention rates in times of increased need.

- The classic over-the-counter antioxidants, vitamin C, E, and beta-carotene, account for only a very small portion of the total antioxidant capacity of fruits and vegetables. Foods contain hundreds, if not thousands, of other healthful chemicals, including antioxidants, that are not available in over-the-counter supplements. And because supplemental antioxidants may have both pro-oxidant and antioxidant potential when taken in supplement form (especially in large dosages), it is far wiser to rely on appropriate food choices than on supplement manufacturers' limited understanding of how these processes work.
- One pound of muscle mass contains roughly 22 percent protein, or 100 grams. The typical nonvegetarian American diet provides more than enough protein for muscle mass development. There have been many demonstrations that supplemental protein is unnecessary for athletes or active adults who are not using steroids.
- Athletes and other active adults are far more likely to have diets deficient in carbohydrates (found in fruits, vegetables, grains, and legumes) and in water than in any other nutrient. Without a sufficient intake of carbohydrates and water, many individuals simply are unable to sustain the physical demands of a particular sport or activity level or training program.

- The body's ability to expand and maintain fat storage is a biological necessity for survival for many people in other parts of the world, but it has become a significant health problem for those of us fortunate enough to live in developed countries where food is plentiful. When this efficient fat storage is combined with inactivity, overeating, and chronically poor food choices, obesity quickly becomes a significant problem.
- Body fat has a high caloric content and little water content, and therefore it takes a great deal of time and consistent effort for most people to lose even a few pounds of excess body fat. Even well trained athletes find it difficult to shed a few unwanted pounds of body fat prior to a competitive event. Weight loss and weight maintenance will always require a long-term commitment to good lifestyle choices.
- The fruits, vegetables, legumes, and grains found in most grocery stores contain all the nutrients the body needs to maintain health and intense training levels.

Finally, let's revisit what might be the most important thing to remember after you've closed this book: If you are consistently making poor food choices and you attempt to make up for missing nutrients with dietary supplements, you will be addressing only a few of the problems associated with your dietary habits. Consider one more example that shows how critical a varied diet of quality foods, including all those important phytochemicals, is to enhancing or improving general health.

Grapes, like most fruits and vegetables, contain a class of compounds called flavonoids that may aid in the prevention of heart disease. In 2001 a group of researchers from the Department of Pharmacology and Medicine, Georgetown University Medical Center studied the benefits of purple grape juice, which contains the flavonoids quercetin, catechin, myricetin, kaempferol, and tannic acid, on cardiovascular disease (*Circulation* 2001; 103:2792).

Investigators wanted to know grape juice's effect on the dilation of blood vessels (vasodilation) and the prevention of blood clots (platelet aggregation), both important in reducing the risk of a heart attack or stroke.

Twenty participants drank approximately two cups of juice a day for two weeks. The researchers noted an approximately 33 percent increase in the total antioxidant capacity of the participants' blood, which they attributed to antioxidants other than the standard vitamin C, E, and beta-carotene. They also discovered that platelet activity decreased, suggesting less clotting and the production of the free radical superoxide was reduced by one-third.

The benefits attributed to the purple grape juice were related to the total mixture of compounds in the juice. When the flavonoids were isolated and given individually, the effect was not as great as when the flavonoids were taken in as a group. It is the *mix* of compounds, not the supplementing with isolated compounds, that provides the best results.

This clearly contradicts the belief held by many individuals that they can eat a bad diet as long as they take a "complete" supplement. No such supplement exists, or ever will, regardless of the supplement industry's trumpeted claims.

Keeping this overview in mind, consider the following simple guidelines for ensuring good nutrition and physical training. Most people can follow these strategies to ensure that they are well nourished and healthy.

General Health and Dietary Guidelines

We gain the greatest health benefits and physical development by consuming a plant-based diet with moderate amounts of animal protein products. However, diet histories of competitive, well-trained athletes and some active adults indicate that most do not consume adequate amounts of quality plant-derived foods, such as fruits, vegetables, whole grains, and legumes. Data on the U.S. population as a whole supports this, indicating that only about 10 percent consume the recommended five servings of fruit and vegetables per day (Ziegler, R. G., 1991; "Vegetables, fruits and carotenoids and the risk of cancer." *Am J Clin Nutr* 53: 251–219). In fact, these foods should make up 50 to 60 percent of the total calories consumed, and they should be the largest food portions eaten at each meal. The American Council on Science and Health recommends the following as a daily diet:

- 6 to 11 servings of bread, cereals, rice, or pasta,
- 3 to 5 servings of vegetables,
- 2 to 4 servings of fruits,
- 2 to 3 servings of dairy products, and
- 2 to 3 servings of meat (chicken, fish, etc.) or a meat substitute.

Bear in mind that caloric needs vary greatly. Recall that without adequate energy intake the maintenance of current muscle mass may be compromised as well as the development of new muscle mass as well. A deficient caloric diet will also negatively affect immune function, and most benefits associated with physical training, such as strength, speed, coordination, increased utilization of body fat for energy, etc.

Total caloric needs are going to be related to age, gender, body size, intensity, duration and frequency of training. As an example, an endurance athlete may need 3,200 to 5,000 calories per day or more. Strength and power athletes caloric needs are going to be comparable due to their significantly greater body size and muscle mass as well as the duration of their intense training levels. An active adult who may only exercise sixty minutes per day would have caloric needs around 2,100 to 3,000 per day.

A fairly simple but crude way to adjust caloric needs is simply the gut/hip check. It does not take a genius to figure out that if your gut or hips are developing at a faster rate than your muscle tissue, it is time to reduce total calories and/or increase training intensity or duration. Let common sense dictate whether or not your average diet is at the low end or the high end of the recommendations provided above by the ACSH; even the lowest number of servings will provide the nutrients necessary to maintaining excellent health and conditioning even if your caloric needs are that limited.

To determine what changes to make in your diet, begin by recording the foods and amounts you eat on five days, including three weekdays plus Saturday and Sunday (since most people eat very differently on weekends than they do during the week). After five days, review your diet history and compare it to the ACSH recommendations above. It should be apparent whether you are consistently consuming adequate fruits, vegetables, and grains.

Using all of the above guidelines, here is a sample healthful daily food menu for an active, normal-weight adult who exercises roughly one hour per day, five to six days per week:

Breakfast: 2 cups juice (orange, grape, or pineapple) 2 slices whole-wheat toast with butter or margarine 2 cups oatmeal with raisins 1 cup nonfat or 1% milk
Snack: apple (or other fruit) and 1–2 slices whole-grain bread
Lunch: sandwich (chicken, fish, turkey, ham, beef, or peanut butter) on whole-wheat bread with 1 large roma tomato, romaine lettuce, mayonnaise, and mustard carrots and 1 cup nonfat or 1% milk
Dinner: baked chicken, fish, or other lean meat or meat substitute (3–4 oz), except on Saturday, which can be reserved for hot dogs, pizza, hamburgers and fries, etc. vegetables (1–2 cups or more) and/or fruit rice or potatoes nonfat milk dessert 3 or 4 nights of the week

This menu is just one example, and meals can vary greatly depending upon daily activity levels. The caloric content or volume of food may almost double for many competitive athletes. What's most important about this menu is that it includes a wide variety of foods and many of them are plant based. If you have to decrease caloric intake because of physical inactivity, the body will adjust nutrient absorption and retention rates to utilize them more efficiently. Conversely, if caloric needs rise, perhaps due to a dramatic increase in activity level, there would be increases in both the availability of nutrients consumed and in increased absorption rates, assuming an increase in food intake. Because of the nutrient balance mechanisms discussed in the vitamin and mineral chapter, your entire nutrient needs will be met in either case.

When you follow this general pattern for selecting foods, the intake of fat and protein combined is approximately 35 to 40 percent of the total caloric intake. Of course, there will be days when you don't reach this proportion, but for the most part you can maintain that level simply by making appropriate food choices at most meals.

To some zealous health enthusiasts, this approach to eating nutritiously may seem like an oversimplification. It is a commonly held view that feeding ourselves healthfully has to be a complex process of weighing and portioning. But the truth is that it can be very simple, once you understand that you can meet the body's basic nutrient needs by making reasonable food choices.

Performance and Training Guidelines

The current energy, nutrient, and fluid recommendations for athletes and other active adults are accurately laid out in the "Key Points" section of the *Joint Position Statement* on *Nutrition and Athletic Performance*, a joint publication of the American College of Sports Medicine (ACSM), the American Dietetic Association (ADA), and

Dietitians of Canada (DC) (*Med Sci Sports Exerc* Vol. 32, No. 12, pp. 2,130–2,145, 2000). They are good general guidelines for anyone committing to good nutrition habits, active lifestyle or serious athletic training. Sport nutrition experts can adjust the recommendations to accommodate the unique concerns of individual athletes, factoring in health, nutrient needs, food preferences, and body weight and composition goals. (I have added my own comments after each of the thirteen key points from the ACSM, ADA, and the DC)

#1: ALWAYS MAINTAIN A HIGH-CARBOHYDRATE DIET

During times of high-intensity training, enough food must be consumed to maintain body weight, maximize training effects, and maintain health. Failure to maintain an adequate intake of calories may result in loss of muscle mass, menstrual dysfunction, loss of or failure to gain bone density, and increased risk of fatigue, injury, and illness.

Comment: As I've noted, a lack of quality carbohydrates is the most limiting factor in the diets of most individuals, especially athletes, and the effects of a carbohydrate deficit are seen in more than just physical performance and development. Bulk up on fruits, grains, and legumes during and between meals. Most athletes notice significant changes in both energy level and strength within seven to fourteen days when they make this adjustment. Also bear in mind that if calories are insufficient for training demands, muscle development will not occur.

#2: MAINTAIN REASONABLE BODY WEIGHT AND COMPOSITION

Body weight and composition do affect performance, but they should not be used as the sole criteria for participation in sports. Daily weigh-ins are discouraged. Optimal body-fat levels vary with sex, age, and heredity, as well as the sport itself. Moreover, body-fat assessment techniques have inherent variability, thus limiting their precision. If weight loss (fat loss) is desired, start early—before the competitive season.

Comment: Although daily weigh-ins are discouraged for body composition purposes, you may find them useful if you are at high risk for dehydration. Do you perspire heavily and find that rehydration within twenty-four hours, or prior to the next training session, is difficult? You could use a daily weigh-in to prevent dehydration. See Chapter 6 for more details.

With regard to body-fat assessment, a good visual check in front of a mirror will provide most athletes with enough information. Bear in mind that many active individuals simply do not function well at a very low level of body fat, nor can they achieve it. Do not succumb to cultural or coaching pressures by setting unrealistic or unnecessary body composition goals. Many athletes—perhaps most individuals—have unrealistic body standards that they haven't the time, ability, genetics, or need to achieve.

Roughly two pounds per week should be the maximum weight loss goal. Any effort to lose more than that would likely require too great a calorie reduction, inhibiting the maintenance of maximum muscle and liver glycogen levels and therefore training and performance. Reduce fat intake prior to any significant changes in carbohydrate intake.

#3: APPROPRIATE TIMING OF CARBOHYDRATE SOURCES

Carbohydrates are important to maintaining blood-glucose levels during exercise and replacing muscle glycogen after exercise. Recommendations for athletes range from 6 to 10 g/kg body weight per day (1 kg = 2.2 pounds; to determine your weight in kilograms, divide your current weight in pounds by 2.2). The amount required depends on the athlete's gender, total daily energy expenditure, the type of sport performed, and environmental conditions.

Comment: Many athletes make the mistake of consuming excessive quantities of sports drinks long after training or competing, believing that they will enhance the recovery of the muscle tissues' energy stores. This is not how these products are meant to be used.

Sports drinks are necessarily low in carbohydrates to allow for rapid passage into the intestinal tract for absorption in order to rehydrate you quickly and assist in the maintenance of blood sugar levels while competing. However, after this rehydration has occurred, you should consume foods and beverages with a higher carbohydrate concentration, such as dried fruit, fruit, fruit juices, nonfat milk, breads, cereals, beans, corn, and potatoes. Those athletes who fail to consume enough calories from carbohydrates and protein within one to two hours after a training session are likely to experience less than optimal muscular recovery for the next day's workout.

You should never rely completely on sports drinks as a post-exercise source of carbohydrates. Their vitamin and mineral content, as well as the complete absence of the necessary phytochemicals make them a poor replacement for food after you have rehydrated.

For many active people, training or competition tends to significantly diminish interest in food for several hours. In these cases, pureed fruit and vegetable drinks like those developed by Bolthouse Farms are a good choice. These products naturally provide fluids, vitamins, minerals, electrolytes, plus many phytochemicals not contained in typical sports drinks.

#4: PROTEIN REQUIREMENTS

Highly active people have slightly increased protein requirements. Protein recommendations for endurance athletes are 1.2 to 1.4 g/kg body weight per day; for resistance and strength-trained athletes they can be as high as 1.6 to 1.7 g/kg body weight per day. These recommended protein intakes can be met through diet alone, without using protein or amino acid supplements, provided that the energy intake is adequate to maintain body weight.

Comment: Recall that one pound of muscle contains only approximately 100 grams of protein. Even if you *could* develop one pound of muscle mass per week—which is not possible unless you use steroids—this would require consuming only 14 to 15 grams of extra protein per day, the equivalent of about two cups of nonfat milk. However, if you feel protein supplements are too much a part of your daily food regimen to give up, let me suggest adding nonfat powdered milk, which provides a well-regulated source of excellent protein and is less expensive than supplements. Some good references feel 1.8 to 2.0 g/kg of body weight may be beneficial for some strength athletes.

#5: FAT REQUIREMENTS

There is no performance benefit in consuming a diet with less than 15 percent of energy from fat, compared with the recommended 20 to 25 percent of energy from fat. Fat is important in athletes' diets because it provides energy, fat-soluble vitamins, and essential fatty acids. (However, there is no scientific basis for recommending high-fat diets to athletes).

Comment: Unsaturated fats from foods such as grains, nuts, oils, and vegetables should make up the bulk of your fat intake. Mixed nuts and raisins or other dried fruit or trail mix is an excellent snack. Many athletes avoid nuts due to their fat content, but nuts contain many chemicals that assist in maintaining your health. For example, walnut polyphenols have antioxidant abilities (*Journal of Nutrition* 2001; 131:2,837–2,842).

#6: CHOOSE NUTRIENT-DENSE FOODS

The athletes at greatest risk of micronutrient deficiency are those who restrict energy intake or use severe weight loss methods. Some individuals will eliminate one or more food groups from their diet or consume high-carbohydrate diets with low micronutrient density. The successful athlete will strive to consume a diet that provides at least the RDAs/RDIs for all micronutrients from food.

Comment: My advice here deviates slightly from the joint paper's recommendation. The RDAs/RDIs are only guidelines that are intended for professionals. It is not necessary to achieve them on a daily basis, although athletes with an above average caloric intake making reasonably wise food choices will achieve this. The mechanisms described in Chapter 3 allow all healthy individuals to maintain nutrient balance over a broad range of daily intakes—even if the intake is often well below the RDAs/RDIs. There are millions of healthy Americans who do not achieve the RDAs daily and who do not use supplements. (The exception might be iron for premenopausal female athletes with heavy menses who consume little animal protein.)

Some vegetarians, particularly athletes or highly active individuals, may be at risk for low-energy, low-protein, and low-micronutrient intakes because of relatively high intakes of low-energy foods and the elimination of meat and dairy from the diet. Consultation with a registered dietician will help avoid these nutrition problems.

#7: MAINTAIN HYDRATION

Dehydration decreases physical performance. That means an adequate fluid intake before, during, and after exercise is necessary for optimal performance and to maintain health. Athletes should drink enough fluid to balance their fluid losses. Two hours before exercise, 400 to 600 ml (14 to 22 oz) of fluid should be consumed, and during exercise 150 to 350 ml (6 to 12 oz) of fluid should be consumed every fifteen to twenty minutes, depending on tolerance. After exercise, an athlete should drink adequate fluid to replace sweat loss incurred during exercise. The recommended amount of fluid replenishment is at least 450 to 675 ml (16 to 24 oz) of fluid for every pound (0.5 kg) of body weight lost during exercise.

Comment: Sports drinks like Gatorade, Powerade, and Accelerade can be very effective for many active individuals, depending on the length of the activity and the amount of body fluid lost. These drinks contain just enough sugar and salt to make them palatable in large amounts. And don't forget water; some people find it easier to consume adequate amounts of water if it's chilled or flavored water (flavor your own by adding lemon or orange slices).

#8: PREGAME OR PREEXERCISE MEALS

A meal or snack before exercise should provide sufficient fluid to maintain hydration. It also should be relatively low in fat and fiber to allow gastric emptying and minimize gastrointestinal distress. It should be relatively high in carbohydrate to maximize maintenance of blood glucose, be moderate in protein, and be composed of food familiar to and well tolerated by the athlete.

Comment: "Before exercise" usually means approximately three hours. This allows time for digestion and absorption. Good choices include beans, fruit, grains, cereals, pasta, pancakes, and sandwiches made from very lean meat, such as chicken, tuna, or turkey. A great precompetition meal might consist of a chicken sandwich (with only a few ounces of chicken) or a peanut butter sandwich; fresh, frozen, or canned fruit; beans; and chocolate or regular nonfat milk. Avoid foods like hamburgers, fries, pizza, chips, and candy—very poor choices because of their high fat content. Athletes who have stomach discomfort due to precompetition anxiety might want to use liquid meals.

If, like some athletes, you simply do not like to eat prior to competition, make an effort the night before both to choose appropriate foods and to increase portion sizes, and thus calories, to compensate for the absence of food the following day.

#9: FOOD AND DRINK DURING EXERCISE

The primary goals for nutrient consumption during exercise are to replace lost fluid and provide carbohydrates (approximately 30 to 60 g/hr) to maintain blood glucose levels. These nutrition guidelines are especially important for athletes involved in endurance events that last more than one hour. The guidelines also apply when an athlete has not consumed adequate food or fluid before exercise or if the athlete is exercising in an extreme environment (heat, cold, or altitude).

Comment: Examples of foods that can be eaten during long periods of activity to obtain the 30 to 60 grams per hour of carbohydrate include:

- raisins: ⅔ cup = 80 grams
- banana: 1 medium = 26 grams
- apple: 1 medium = 21 grams
- orange: 1 medium = 16 grams

Sports drinks can also be very useful for those undertaking endurance events.

#10: MEALS AFTER TRAINING OR COMPETING

After exercise, the dietary goal is to provide adequate energy and carbohydrates to replace muscle glycogen and promote rapid physical recovery. When an athlete is glycogen depleted after exercise, a carbohydrate intake of 1.5 g/kg body weight during the first thirty minutes, and again every two hours for four to six hours, is adequate to replace glycogen stores. Protein consumed after exercise provides amino acids for repair and building of muscle tissue. For that reason, athletes should consume a mixed meal that contains carbohydrates, protein, and fat soon after a strenuous competition or training session.

Comment: The rationale for consuming a high-carbohydrate and moderate-protein meal after training is to stimulate increased levels of insulin in the blood. This hormone stimulates the transport of blood sugars and amino acids from protein digestion into the muscle cells. Theoretically, it also assists in inhibiting the breakdown of established muscle fibers by inhibiting an excessive rise in the hormone cortisol, which stimulates the breakdown of stored carbohydrate, fat, and protein for energy use. This may enhance muscle development and produce a demonstrated improvement in muscle energy recovery in the form of glycogen over the next twenty-four hours. However, keep in mind that very little protein (6 to 10 grams) is needed for this theoretical effect.

More importantly for athletes who train twice a day, research has shown that consuming a high-carbohydrate meal or foods immediately after a training session, compared to two hours later, results in a glycogen resynthesis two times greater than in those athletes who waited two hours to eat. So do not delay. A good post-training or postcompetition meal might consist of lean meat; a baked potato, beans, rice, or corn (several portions, depending on need); a vegetable salad; nonfat or low-fat milk, and dessert.

To calculate more specifically your carbohydrate and protein needs immediately after strenuous training and up to three to four hours later, use the following formulas:

- For carbohydrates: consume .8 to 1.0 grams for every kilogram (2.2 pounds) of body weight.
- For protein: consume roughly .2 grams for every kilogram (2.2 pounds) of body weight.

Many find it convenient to consume a "meal-replacement" beverage after training. While these products can quickly add well-balanced calories when there isn't time to eat a regular meal, remember that you get many more benefits from food. Usually all it takes is some planning and preparation to have appropriate foods available that are relatively easy to consume, such as:

- fresh fruit, fruit juices, dried fruit, or canned fruit,
- canned corn or beans,
- cereal, bagels, whole-grain breads, tortillas,
- a lean meat sandwich,
- and nonfat or low-fat milk.

#11: VITAMIN AND MINERAL SUPPLEMENTS

As a general rule, no vitamin and mineral supplements should be required if an athlete is consuming adequate energy from a variety of foods to maintain body weight. Supplementation recommendations unrelated to exercise—such as folic acid in pregnant women—should be followed. When is a multivitamin/mineral supplement appropriate? When an athlete is dieting, eliminating foods or food groups, is ill or recovering from injury, or when there is a specific micronutrient deficiency, a multivitamin/mineral supplement may be useful. No single nutrient supplements should be used without a specific medical or nutritional reason (e.g., iron supplements to reverse iron deficiency anemia).

Comment: My opinions differ on just one point from those expressed in the joint paper. I do not see a need for supplementation to recover from an injury or illness; no matter whether the injury is to bone, tendon, or muscle, a good diet will provide all that is necessary. In fact, in this scenario the nutrient requirements may lessen, since training will be dramatically reduced in an injured athlete. Unless a need has been medically diagnosed, male athletes and postmenopausal females should never consume a supplement that contains iron because of its potential toxicity. (However, since iron deficiency is a very common problem among female athletes, having a doctor check your iron status may be a wise decision.) Sexually active female athletes should understand that anemia can reduce their ability to absorb folate, which would become a significant issue in pregnancy.

Vitamin supplements will raise the level of the vitamin in the blood, but this will not have any effect on the tissues themselves. As an example, a study in 2002 demonstrated that distance runners supplementing with 1,500 mg of vitamin C for a week before a race had higher blood levels of vitamin C. However, compared to a group of distance runners not receiving the supplement, there were no benefits relating to oxidative or immune changes (Nieman, D. et al. 2002. "Influence of vitamin C supplementation on oxidative and immune changes after an ultramarathon." *J Appl Physiol* 92 (5):1,070–77).

Another study, in which runners ingested 1,000 IU of vitamin E as well as 1,000 mg of vitamin C for four weeks, failed to show any benefit in the prevention of muscle damage (Dawson, D. et al. 2002. "Effect of C and E supplementation on biochemical and ultrastructural indices of muscle damage after a 21 km run." *In J Sports Med* 23 (1):10–15).

#12: ERGOGENIC AIDS

Athletes should be counseled regarding the use of ergogenic aids. In general, they should be used with caution and only after careful evaluation of the product for safety, efficacy, potency, and legality.

Comment: I have discussed at length the safety and efficacy issues regarding many supplements. By now it should be quite clear that the adage "let the buyer beware" is tailor-made for the sports supplement marketplace.

The late Edmund Burke PhD, past Professor and Director, Exercise Science Program University of Colorado, Colorado Springs, and former Coordinator of Sports Sciences, U.S. Olympic Cycling Team also noted that there are several ways an inadvertent doping outcome can arise from supplement use. In some instances, the supplement lists a banned substance among its ingredients on the label, but the consumer is unaware that the substance is banned or that it can produce a positive doping test. In other cases, the supplement contains banned substances that are not listed on the label; the manufacturer might knowingly have included these ingredients, or they might have been inadvertently added as a by-product of other ingredients or as the result of contamination during production. Mislabeling (whether intentional or not) is a problem in the supplement industry, leading many consumers to risk not only positive doping results but serious health consequences.

#13 VEGETARIAN ATHLETES

Vegetarian athletes may be at risk for low energy, protein, and micronutrient intakes because of high intakes of low-energy-dense foods and elimination of meat and dairy from the diet.

Comment: Of particular concern for the vegetarian athlete would be the absence of quality iron sources. These athletes tend to have low iron stores.

Some Notes on Training at Altitude

At 2,000 feet or higher, some athletes may experience problems associated with dehydration, insufficient carbohydrate or sugar storage, and anemia. The United States Olympic Committee publication *Olympic Coach,* in its August 2000 issue, provided the following guidelines and advice for those training at altitude.

The tendency to breathe more deeply and more often at high elevations increases respiratory water loss, exacerbating dehydration. There have also been reports of higher urinary water loss at altitude. Athletes training at elevation may need to consume more water or sports drinks than they would at sea level.

The lower concentration of oxygen in the air at elevation decreases the body's oxygen utilization, which means that muscle mass must rely more heavily on stored carbohydrates. Therefore, it is extremely important to increase the intake of carbohydrates from food when training at altitude.

Female athletes with a tendency to be borderline anemic at sea level will probably have greater performance problems at higher elevations. As the elevation increases, training will cause an increased production of red blood cells to carry oxygen to the working muscles. If the necessary iron is not available to promote this red blood cell production, the synthesis of new red blood cells will not take place. If you are anemic or borderline anemic, and regardless of whether you train at sea level or at altitude, have your doctor check your ferritin levels (ferritin is an indicator of stored iron found in the serum of the blood) to determine if you would benefit from an iron supplement. Bear in mind, however, that a low ferritin level in female athletes is normally attributed to poor iron intake. It can result from chronically eating less than 2,000 calories per day, eating vegetarian or low-meat diets, and limiting iron-fortified foods like breakfast cereals and bread.

A study reported in the *Journal of Applied Physiology* (2000; 84 (3): 1,103–1,111) found that iron supplementation might help improve muscle oxidation capacity in women with low ferritin levels. And an April 2002 report in the *American Journal of Clinical Nutrition* also provided evidence that nonanemic women with significantly reduced or depleted iron stores may have impaired adaptations to training, even at sea level (Vol. 75, No. 4, 734–742). The diagnosis and treatment of anemia should always be monitored by a physician.

* * *

The take-home message is that proper food choices will always be the only healthful way to live. If you follow some fairly simple diet and fitness guidelines, you'll have no reason to embrace the many myths and misconceptions promoted by sport and nutrition supplement companies. You should now be fairly well prepared to navigate the quagmire of misinformation and to objectively determine what applies to your life and lifestyle. What you once considered science, you can now identify as junk science. What you once saw as a health benefit, you now know could be a health threat. And what you once thought was a dietary necessity, you now know will be unnecessary as long as you consistently make good choices and take responsibility for your physical health.

There are no helpful alternative potions that will negate the actions of chronic undisciplined behavior. That said, I note that there are many who are simply more comfortable—for whatever reason—when taking a vitamin/mineral supplement. To minimize any potential disruption of the body's nutrient balance, choose one that does not exceed 100 percent of the RDA for any nutrient, and take it only every two or three days. Males or postmenopausal women should not take any supplement with iron unless it is prescribed by a physician.

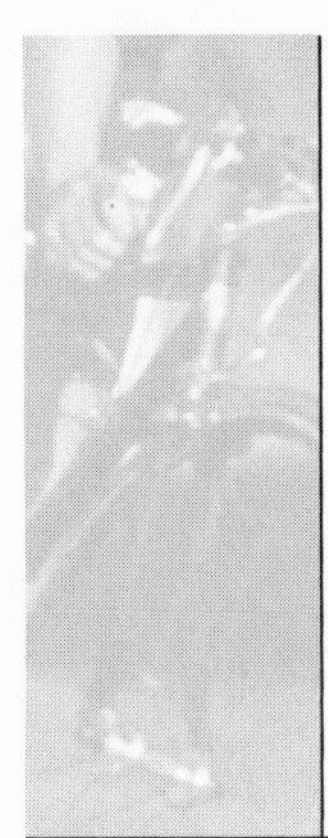

RESOURCES

Reputable Sports Nutrition Information Sites

American College of Sports Medicine
www.acsm.org

The NCAA
www.ncaa.org

Gatorade Sports Science Institute
www.gssiweb.com

Professional Organizations

American Dietetic Association
www.eatright.org

American Society for Clinical Nutrition
www.faseb.org/ascn

American College of Sports Medicine
www.acsm.org

American Society of Nutritional Sciences
www.asns.org

International Life Sciences Institute
www.ilsi.org

National Academy of Sciences/National Research Council
(NAS/NRC)
www.nas.edu

Society for Nutrition Education
www.sne.org

American Cancer Society
www.cancer.org

American Diabetes Association
www.diabetes.org

American Heart Association
www.americanheart.org

Arthritis Foundation
www.arthritis.org

Food and Nutrition Board
National Research Council
National Academy of Sciences
www.nas.edu

American Medical Association
www.ama-assn.org

Reputable Consumer Education and Advocacy Groups

American Council on Science and Health
www.acsh.org

National Council Against Health Fraud
www.ncahf.org

Quackwatch
www.quackwatch.org

Consumers Union
www.consumersunion.org

ConsumerLab
www.ConsumerLab.com

Produce Marketing Association
www.aboutproduce.com

Books for Basic Nutrition Information (Introductory College Texts)

Nutrition Concepts and Controversies
Authors: Francis Sizer and Ellie Whitney
Publisher: Thompson/Wadsworth
ISBN 0-534-64506-2

Contemporary Nutrition
Authors: Gordon Wardlow and Anne Smith
Publisher: McGraw Hill
ISBN 0-07-250185-5

Nutrition Newsletters and Web Site News

Tufts University Diet and Nutrition Letter
www.healthletter.tufts.edu/

Harvard Medical School Health Letter
www.hms.harvard.edu/news/index.html

Mayo Clinic Health Letter
www.mayohealth.org

WebMD
www.WebMD.com

U.S. Government Sites

Center for Disease Control and Prevention's Current
Health Related Hoaxes and Rumors
www.cdc.gov/hoax_rumors.htm

Federal Trade Commission
www.ftc.gov

Federal Trade Commission's Operation Cure All
www.ftc.gov/opa/2001/06/cureall.htm

Food and Drug Administration
www.fda.gov

U.S. Department of Agriculture
www.usda.gov

FDA Center for Food Safety & Applied Nutrition
www.cfsan.fda.gov

Food and Nutrition Information Center, National Agricultural Library
www.nal.usda.gov/fnic

The National Library of Medicine
www.nlm.nih.gov

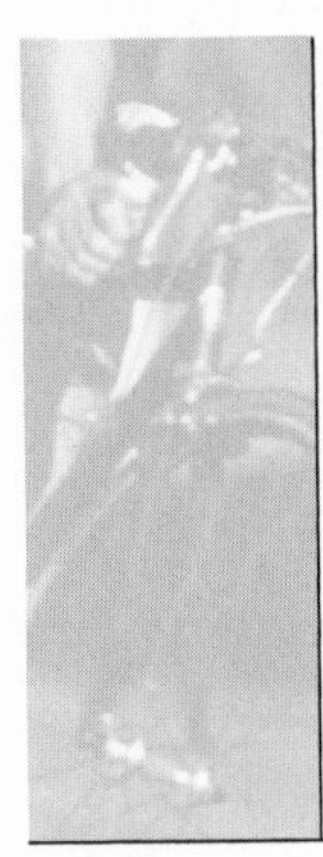

ABOUT THE AUTHOR

David Lightsey, MS has worked on the national level with the non-profit consumer advocacy organization the National Council Against Health Fraud (www.ncahf.org) combating misinformation in the sports nutrition and health marketplace since 1988. He is also a nutrition and food science advisor to the award-winning consumer advocacy Web site Quackwatch (www.Quackwatch.org), is a speaker listed with the NCAA Health and Safety Speakers Grant program, and has been employed in the physical rehabilitation/sports medicine field for the last eighteen years.

Lightsey has appeared on *Dateline NBC* as an expert in the deceptive marketing methods used by the sport supplement industry, as well as *CBS Evening News* regarding the designer steroid scandal. Many other national-level media, university, peer review journals, and professional athletic organizations have utilized his work or his opinion, including ESPN's *Outside The Lines* investigative report on Andro-6, *ABC News Prime Time Live, CBS This Morning*, CNN, the Associated Press, *San Francisco Examiner*, *Washington Post*, the New

York Department of Consumer Affairs, *The Lancet*, *National Strength and Conditioning Association Journal*, *Circulation*, *American Journal of Emergency Medicine*, the San Francisco 49ers, and various law firms.

Lightsey has lectured on nutrition quackery and sports nutrition issues for coaches' clinics, the Bureau of Land Management Hot Shot Fire Crews, the National Athletic Trainers Association, universities, and business meetings.

Two nationally recognized consumer advocates, Stephen Barrett MD and Victor Herbert MD, JD state the following in their book *The Vitamin Pushers: How The Health Food Industry Is Selling America a Bill of Goods* when referring to his work on the deceptive marketing methods used to sell sport supplements: "The most thorough investigation has been conducted by David Lightsey, an exercise physiologist and nutritionists who coordinates the National Council Against Health Frauds Task Force on Ergogenic Aids."

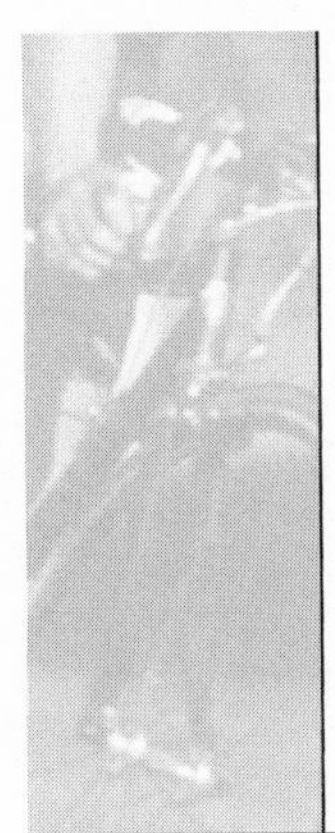

INDEX